GREG McC

FORESKIN'S LAMENT

NEW ZEALAND PLAYSCRIPTS

GENERAL EDITOR: JOHN THOMSON

Glide Time by Roger Hall
Middle Age Spread by Roger Hall
Awatea by Bruce Mason
The Pohutukawa Tree by Bruce Mason
The Two Tigers by Brian McNeill
State of the Play by Roger Hall
Jack Winter's Dream by James K. Baxter
Foreskin's Lament by Bruce Mason
Blood of the Lamb by Bruce Mason
Fifty-Fifty by Roger Hall
Hot Water by Roger Hall
Outside In by Hilary Beaton
The End of the Golden Weather by Bruce Mason
Out in the Cold by Greg McGee
Tooth and Claw by Greg McGee
Shuriken by Vincent O'Sullivan
Objection Overruled by Carolyn Burns
Wednesday to Come by Renée
Driftwood by Rachel McAlpine
Pass It On by Renée
Coaltown Blues by Mervyn Thompson
&
Bruce Mason Solo (hardcover)

In preparation:

Takirima (Five Plays) by Bruce Mason

FORESKIN'S LAMENT

Greg McGee

Victoria University Press

VICTORIA UNIVERSITY PRESS
Victoria University of Wellington
Private Bag Wellington

© *Greg McGee 1981*
ISBN 0 86473 031 4

First published 1981
Reprinted 1982, 1985, 1987

Permission to perform this play must be obtained from **PLAYMARKET**, Post Office Box 9767, Courtenay Place, Wellington, New Zealand. The publishers acknowledge the assistance and advice of **PLAYMARKET**, which was established in 1973 to provide services for New Zealand playwrights.

This play is published
with the aid of grants
from the
New Zealand Literary Fund
and Playmarket

National Library of New Zealand
Cataloguing-in-Publication data
McGEE, Greg, 1950-
  Foreskin's Lament / Greg McGee. — Wellington
[N.Z.] : Victoria University Press, 1985. —
1 v. — (New Zealand playscripts)
  A play for 2 women and 7 men. —
First published Wellington, N.Z. : Price Milburn :
Victoria University Press, 1981.
  ISBN 0-86473-031-4
        NZ822.2
  I. Title. II. Series.

Printed in Hong Kong through Bookprint
Consultants Ltd, Wellington

Contents

Foreword by Michael Neill....................	9
First Performance	18
Author's Note.............................	19
Characters	20
Foreskin's Lament	21

For Joan and Bill

Foreword

A lament is an act of mourning; for Greg McGee's Gaelic ancestors it named a pipe air, the dirge for a dead hero. *Foreskin's Lament* mourns the end of heroes, the passing of an age. In the long speech which concludes the play, the formal lament from which it takes its title, Foreskin invokes the legends of his tribe, its heroic lore:

> for a whole generation god was only twice as high as the posts. We who know our history by itineraries — the cold war of the '50s you say? Oh yes, we remember it well, those front-row problems, Skinner and Bekker. '59? A melange of O'Reilly's creamy thighs, Jackson's jink, DB's size 13s, and a sheep-dog retrieving the ball in a cow-paddock in Morrinsville. Froggies in '61, Poms again in '66 — bloody awful! — those artistes of '68, Villepreux and Jo Maso, a Pinetree bestriding the '60s with a sheep under each arm, the Bokkies in '73 — the ones that didn't come, that never more will come . . . there was one thing we knew with certainty: come winter, we'd be there, on the terrace, answering the only call that mattered — c'mon black! . . . while the nectar flowed till you could almost see the reflection of your youth in its dregs . . . passing . . . passing. I know the lore, I know the catechism.

To the generation for which McGee (the former All Black trialist) speaks, the lore was Law, the Rugby Code a Covenant, and football grounds the shrines of tribal custom. But Foreskin's lament is the plaint of a man who finds himself strangely 'unaccustomed', for whom the myths, with all their remembered potency have lost their magic. When myths no longer serve to incarnate the values of a people, the customs that declare its sense of family, they become the maudlin properties of a lying nostalgia. McGee's players dream of epic glory — like Andy Haden thrashing Wales with his broken hand:

> KOed out of your scone last week, hero this week!
> This is the stuff of rugby, this is how legends are made!

But in the demythologised world announced by Clean, where Tupper, the 'rip-shit-or-bust coach', represents 'a dying breed', 'just an old fart left over from the Second World War', legends lose their glow. 'Twenty or thirty years from now' Foreskin says of Clean 'he'll just be a big, fat, dumb heavy, living on delusions of former glory and free beers from fans with long memories . . . looking for immortality in the dregs of every glass'. 'Twenty years . . . ten years . . . in a couple of years', the predictions sound through the play like a melancholy refrain. Only a people which has lost faith in its past fears for its future.

So *Foreskin's Lament* is not just a play about rugby, but (as its workshop producer, Mervyn Thompson, put it), a play about 'the state of the nation', A.D. 1980. It is identifiably set in 1976, but if we have known our history by itineraries, then we shall also remember 1980 as the year in which the Rugby Union drew up its secret itinerary for a Springbok tour and turned its back on history. What Greg McGee's play has to show us is that it was never possible to keep politics out of rugby, because in New Zealand (as in South Africa) rugby has been an expression of the *polis*: 'This is a team game, son, and the town is the team. It's the town's honour at stake when the team plays, god knows there's not much else around here.' 'The town *is* the team' — Tupper's line is almost a paraphrase of *Coriolanus,* 'The people *are* the city', but it practically inverts that democratic slogan. In Tupper's book the town exists only insofar as it is defined by the team: the 'common goal' of his social ideal is entirely self-referential — simply 'that sense of comradeship' which comes from the submission of the individual to the common desire for victory. 'The point of the bloody game . . . is to win' he insists: *what* is to be won doesn't matter, the goal is simply to have a goal. McGee does not cheaply dismiss Tupper's brand of stoic romanticism, his vision of a game which is 'a test of guts and character, not skill' through which 'a man, an ordinary bloke, can find out a lot about himself and his mates'. Indeed McGee's most affectionate (as well as his funniest) writing goes into the creation of the aging coach whose passion for the game as 'the finest thing I've ever experienced' later sweeps him into inarticulate lyricism:

> You're an army man yourself Clean, you know what I'm talking about, camder — ah, you know, the old camerder — ah, comradeship, the common cause.

But it's exactly McGee's affection for Tupper and the ideal of laconic mateship for which he stands, which gives the play's questioning of old shibboleths its hard (and finally uncompromising) edge. Challenged by Foreskin to argue the question of goals, Tupper simply denies its relevance: for him strength is a matter of silence — of *not* asking the questions:

FORESKIN: How can we be mates? . . . We don't agree on anything important.
TUPPER: Important? Important my arse. The best mates I've ever had, we never got past the time of day. What's important? You just get on with it.

'You just get on with it' — and then where do you get? If the old myths have failed us, if that stoical expression of national self-survival 'just get on with it' — has become the slogan of a willed self-ignorance, then McGee wants to know why.

The imaginative hold of rugby on a man like Tupper has less to do with the playing field as a training ground for heroes, than with the club as a kind of surrogate family. It's not for nothing that Tupper calls his players 'son', or that Foreskin (only half-satirically) calls him 'dad'. For Larry the team replaces the wife and child who left him: 'I like to be a part of it, I've no family or anything.' If the club-family provides a refuge in which Larry can shelter and sublimate his homosexuality, for the other players it offers the prospect of an indefinitely extended adolescence of masculine camaraderie. On the field, in the showers, men of 29, in flight from adult responsibilities envisaged as suburban nightmare ('a wife, a couple of screaming kids and mortgaged to the tonsils'), can still be 'the boys, the lads'. Even for the self-seeking Clean, with his commercialised cult of personality ('Once you've made the name, you can travel on it.'), the club still provides a nexus of security, like the army or the police: 'You obey orders . . . You're looked after, no worries'. For its other members, the team is not just a haven of male security, but the emotional centre of their existence promising (according to Tupper) 'the highest, best thing that most of these lads will ever experience in their lives', feeding all those 'grand emotions' missing in the 'smaller game' called life. The ironic paradox McGee pursues is that a society, whose predominantly calvinist ethic has systematically discouraged the public display of emotion and the recognition of emotional contact, should discover its self-image in the extravagant contact sport of rugby. Irish makes the point with characteristically sardonic humour:

> It's so bloody boring. Push, pull your head out, run about till you find another heap of fellas, find a hole to stick your head in where it's dark, push again, pull it out, run along to the next heap.

McGee is not making the obvious gibe about locker-room homosexuality — though the game of mock-buggery with which Clean and Irish humiliate Larry exposes the extent to which repressed homosexual feeling feeds their cruelty and contempt. But this is part of a larger theme, the play's concern with a society emotionally stunted by hatred of its own sexuality. The innocent rugby childhood which Foreskin mourns includes 'times of closeness, father and son, brother and weary brother, waking very early on cold mornings, huddling together under a blanket in front of a wireless. ...' But the contacts are all male: fathers, sons and brothers, united in the surrogate orgasm of conversion — '*wait* for it, *wait* for it!'; while the game itself is remembered as escape from the mother, the engulfing threat of female emotion:

> I was born of the same mothers as you — all! I was part of a whole generation that grew up on wintry mornings running from between mum's warm coat ends on to dewy green fields. ... away ... from all that attention.

Kenny, stretched out by Clean's kick in the head, feels 'like a real girl'; forwards who won't go over the top of a man play like 'a pack of poofters'. The insults are not casual, but voice the deepest fears of a male-dominated society which has learnt to despise its own feelings ('we were taught not to cry a vale of tears ago') — a society which attempts to control its fears by objectifying homosexuals as 'poofs' and women as 'fluff'. This is the ethos which imagines women's sex as an alarming 'gash that never heals' (an image combining fear and disgust with the threat of sadistic violence), and which projects the male member as an innocent and vulnerable child — poor 'wee

Arnold' who needs to be taken 'for a trot', for all the world like some schoolboy rep. Women are seen as predatory beasts whose sole aim in life is to get some helpless man to 'chuck a rock' so that they may trap him once again in the old prison of emotional demand. Larry's recollected fear of a woman's demands is matched and even exceeded, ironically enough, by those very aggressive males whose seemingly confident sexuality he envies. It's the intervention of Moira in the second act which most forcefully points up this irony: in the presence of a woman who declines to conform to the assigned role of 'fluff' Tupper develops a defenceless pathos, Clean becomes openly defensive. Before her gaze both appear more profoundly naked than in the changing room of Act I. Yet McGee is too good a dramatist to simply endorse her easy dismissal of Tupper and Clean as 'anachronistic pigs'. Clean's brutal intelligence shows up the limitations of Moira's comfortable liberalism, as effectually as her urbane wit exposes his diseased sexual chauvinism.

One of the play's strengths is the clarity with which it reveals the coarse and violent language of masculine camaraderie as an expression of intense sex-hatred: 'fuck' and 'cunt' are terms of abuse for precisely the same reasons that Clean persistently associates women and shit. Women are shit because they corrupt the 'pure' male world for which rugby stands; the obscene jocosity of the shower song makes just this point:

And when she's dead and long forgotten . . .
I'll dig her up and fuck her rotten.

That is what being 'heavily into fluff' means for Clean: sex as self-violation. It's bitterly appropriate therefore that the action on which the plot turns should itself be a kind of self-violation — Clean's murderous assault on his own captain. The rhetoric of sexual violence corresponds, at a deep level, to the rhetoric of rugby violence. Tupper's refrain makes the connection: 'Play the *fucken* game'. Rugby, he insists, is a game for men, (like 'entertainment for men'?) a game whose principal aim is to score, and whose finest 'strategy' is to 'kick shit out of everything'. Of course *rhetoric* is just what it is, play-acting — like the sexual bravado which is supposed to sort the men from the boys (girls?). As Tupper explains with touching ingenuousness: 'A coach must be a bit of an actor — for psychological reasons'. And the brilliant vignette in which he flounders his way through a mountain of cheerios and pavlova to use 'a bit of the old sly' with Moira comically reveals the boy behind the man. Language, however, has a nasty way of compelling reality: play with a metaphor long enough and someone will start to take it literally. Clean, in the end, is as much Tupper's son as Foreskin. However affectionately McGee regards his 'old bull' — and Foreskin comes to feel that they are 'on the same side' — Tupper must nevertheless take the responsibility for Kenny's death. Clean is the Monster to Tupper's Frankenstein then; but he is also a monster of our own creation, in a country whose elected leadership uses the nostalgic language of a Tupper ('just ordinary blokes, the salt of the earth') to mask the ethics of a Clean ('everything's there for the taking'). Foreskin insists that we, with Moira, see it:

> This is the heart and the bowels of this country, too strong and foul and vital for reduction to bouquets, or oils, or words. If you think they're pigs, then you'd better look closer, and get used to the smell, because their smell is your smell.

Clean is the boy who came back from the 'bloody good war' which is Tupper's solution to the ills of this society. Vietnam too was 'a battle worth winning', something you 'just got on with'.

'Coming back' is an important theme in the play — whether one thinks of Clean coming back from the Nam, or Moira coming back from her O.E., or Foreskin coming back to Kaitaki ('my earth') from the university. It's going away and coming back which gives these three characters their peculiar perspective on the team and the community values for which it stands. Unlike those true outsiders, Irish and Larry, who camouflage their alienation by 'playing the game' and submitting to the corporate blindness of the ruck, Clean, Moira and Foreskin have their eyes open. Clean and Moira, in their opposite ways, both repudiate the values of the team: Moira, for all her sharpness of wit, merely mouths the individualist clichés of 'European' liberalism; Clean clings desperately to the slogans of 'American' self-help, the lessons that he (like Reagan's supporters) gleaned from Indo-China:

FOREWORD

those yanks are the boys. They've got it by the balls. You stick it to them, that's their philosophy. Right up the arse. You stick it to them till they've got turds coming out their nostrils.

They illustrate the failings of two kinds of individualism. Foreskin, on the other hand, is a man in the middle; caught between his commitment to the tradition for which Tupper, with all his deficiencies, stands, and his suspicion of the mindless herd-politics which worship of the 'team' can produce. With Tupper he challenges the assumption that the individual should lose himself in the team:

> Who is the team, Tupper? What is the team? There's just a collection of human beings. The team has no magical properties of its own.

To Moira he insists on the worth of the tribal legends. Moira believes that people must learn to 'really be themselves', Tupper maintains that this 'just confuses people. Man wants to know where he stands.' Foreskin's notion of identity includes both; to be yourself, you must know where you stand:

> It's not a competition Moira. You're not enough. They're not enough. But that's not even the point. This is my earth. I'm rooted in it, whatever my fine aspirations.

So coming back, for Foreskin, is a question of discovering where you stand and asserting who you are. It's an old ideal of balance: not unlike the one that Dr Arnold thought his school's game would develop. But in Foreskin's world it's a balance not easily maintained. Tupper's ethos is one that insists on the suspension of mind and individuality in the cause of what he takes to be the common good: typically he believes in a forward game, where the job of the backs is to keep the ball in front of the forwards, while the job of the forwards is to 'kick shit out of everything above grass height'. Good forwards should be 'like those pit ponies, blind from lack of light', and Tupper's ingrained suspicion of backs stems from the fact that they can see too much back there ('gaps I couldn't squeeze my doodle into'). Seeing, for him, amounts to detachment, detachment to lack of involvement: 'Tupper is the kind of coach who likes the captain to be a forward, a leader who's more involved, a leader by example'. Foreskin's position at fullback is the sign of his detachment. Of all those who have learnt to see, he is the one (as his christian name suggests) who sees most; and in the end he sees too much.

> You see a lot from my position Tupper. . . . Kenny got kicked in the head twice by the same player, yet we were playing different teams each time — well, that really takes the cake. Do you see how truly funny that is?

Foreskin's Lament is a dirge for Foreskin's world, but it is also a lament for Foreskin's own innocence, finally destroyed with that one Clean kick. When Foreskin tells Moira he's 'mourning [for] a rugby player I used to know', he's thinking of himself as much as Kenny. But if the play is an act of mourning, it also enacts an initiation ceremony — the moral and emotional circumcision which Foreskin himself describes:

FORESKIN: Progress has a lot of chops to answer for — trees, animals, sensibilities of all kinds, what's a piece of skin?
MOIRA: Can cover a lot of sensibilities. . . .
FORESKIN: Lost. Pretersensual pain — the chop I missed and have always been bound for.

Clean's kick delivers the chop: but it's only a prepuce that's left on his sprig, not the severed cock of Foreskin's nightmares. The final litany of mourning sets the catechism of rugby against the rival creed of Foreskin's education. Neither, as he warned Moira, is enough: if one set of myths is discredited, the other seems borrowed and fraudulent. The heroes of Foreskin's alternative mythology (Perelman, Bowie, Kubrick, Burroughs, Kerouac, Cleaver) may have helped to show him who he is, but they cannot tell him where he stands, since they are not of 'my earth'; the lamented heroes of the tribe (Skinner, Clarke, Jarden, Jones, Stewart, Tremain), though they may tell him where he's come from, can no longer show him where he stands:

> I escaped from all that — I think that's probably where I left you. I went from here and wandered . . .
> where the hell was I?
> Ah, but I came back . . .
> And now the dance is done. I'm hanging up my boots — whaddarya?

FOREWORD

The dilemma that McGee asks us to face is in some sense the dilemma which faces all provincial societies: how to escape provinciality without submitting to debilitating definition by 'the other', 'someone else's [resonance]'. It is not enough just to see more than all those blind 'fronts': to see yourself, you must learn to see *for* yourself, not simply to reconstruct the world as others have made it. To the problem of identity the play offers no answers; but it puts the question with an urgency and power that make it a genuine initiation: *'Whaddarya? Whaddarya? Whaddarya?* . . .'. Foreskin beats his head against the word; and that particular pack-snarl, with all its force of hatred, contempt and naked fear, will never sound quite the same again — it separates the men from the boys all right.

MICHAEL NEILL

First performance

FORESKIN'S LAMENT was first performed by Theatre Corporate, Auckland, on 30 October 1980, when the cast was as follows:

FORESKIN	Christopher White
TUPPER	Roy Billing
CLEAN	Grant McFarland
IRISH	Philip Holder
MOIRA	Judy Gibson
LARRY	John Watson
MEAN	Geoffrey Snell
KEN	Gregory Naughton
PAT	Alison Quigan

Directed by Roger McGill
Designed by John Verryt
Personal assistant to Director, Alison Quigan
Stage Manager, Simon Garrett
Set Construction by Gary Reading

Author's note

The text that follows is much as it appeared in the Theatre Corporate production. I have re-instated certain Corporate cuts, on the specious excuse that each production will present intrinsic difficulties, and therefore ought to have the benefit of a 'basic' text.

The chrysalis of any play, that between-first-and-last-draft stage, probably owes much to many people. I would like to record my gratitude for Theatre Corporate's faith and dedication. A first production also involves a thorough session of script editing, and in this respect I was very fortunate to have the guidance of Raymond Hawthorne particularly, and Roger McGill. The development of the play owes a tremendous amount also to the New Zealand Playwrights' Workshop organised by Playmarket in Wellington, to the intense, co-operative atmosphere there, and to Mervyn Thompson in particular.

Players:

FORESKIN — Fullback. Student. More delicate in physique than the others, nevertheless athletic. Of modern aspect in style, longish hair.

KEN — First five-eighth, and captain. A building contractor, shortish, but solid.

CLEAN — Prop, and vice-captain. A policeman. Must be of acceptable prop dimensions, well built, thick neck, hair-cut and dress compromise modern.

MEAN — Lock. Farmer, taller and slimmer than Clean, nevertheless powerfully built. Clean-cut with agricultural sideboards.

IRISH — No. 8. Reasonably tall, angular. Strong remains of an Irish accent.

Coach:

TUPPER — Ex-prop. Middle-aged, paunch of impressive dimensions, loud voice.

Manager/Masseur:

LARRY — Branch manager. Fiftyish, small, neat.

Characters: (additional to those appearing in Act One)

MOIRA — Lawyer. Elegant. Twenty-five to thirty.

PAT — Mean's wife. Homely, thirtyish.

The play is in two Acts. Act I takes place in a rugby changing room on a Thursday evening. Act II takes place at a party at Larry's house the following Saturday night.

Act One

Set — *Dim light. The inside of a dressing shed. Floor and walls of bare boards. Clothes are hanging along two walls left and right. Low forms below the clothes, with shoes, socks stowed under them. In the backstage wall, two wooden doors. The word 'shower' is etched crudely in white paint above the door on the left. Centrestage, with assorted bottles of liniment and rubbing-oil on it, is a long wooden table. There is a strong smell of liniment. Old socks, jockstraps, boots, balls, and a couple of beer bottles are littered about.*

From off-stage, a loud bull-horn voice.

TUPPER: Get excited about it! Go over the top of him, don't hang off! Use your bloody feet, you pack of poofters. Ruck! Ruck! You won't hurt him, you won't hurt him, I guarantee it!

Pause

Oh shit.

Pause

Now come on Kenny lad, get up, don't just lie there, it can't be that bad. Come on, on your feet, play the game son. They're not dishing out any Oscars tonight, you know.

Pause

Oi! Mean, Irish! Come over here and take him away. No, you won't need that stretcher Larry, a couple of the lads will help carry him. Just needs a bit of a rub-down, don't you, Kenny?

During the following speech: Lights. IRISH *and* MEAN, *in dirty rugby gear, carry* KEN, *similarly dressed, on stage through the unmarked door.* KEN'S *arms are draped over the other two players' shoulders. Behind them, like a mother hen, comes* LARRY, *dressed in ordinary trousers and a colourful track-suit top over a business shirt.*

Right! The rest of you bastards mind where you're putting your bloody great feet — you're meant to be kicking shit out of the opposition, not our guys. Keep an eye open for the ball while you're at it.
Okay, we'll take it from a set scrum over here on the right. We're going to spin it to the left. Foreskin will be coming into the line outside centre, he'll drop it — on purpose this time! — and we'll have the loose forwards out there to tidy up as quick as a wink of my Aunt Fanny's twat. No shirking, let's finish with a bit of guts — whaddarya anyway?

LARRY: Just put him there on the table. Easy does it, my lads . . . there.

LARRY *supports* KEN'S *legs as* IRISH *and* MEAN *sit him on the table with both legs flat in front of him.* KEN *is facing up-stage.*

Now, let's have a good look at it, Kenny.

IRISH *and* MEAN *sit down on the forms and watch with interest as* LARRY *begins feeling* KEN'S *leg.* IRISH *rustles about in his bag for a cigarette.*

LARRY: Come on, you two, out you go. The Tupper will be having chickens.
IRISH: Jesus, do we have to? All this extra training isn't good for me. The fitter I get, the more effort it takes to get exhausted.
MEAN: That's Irish.
IRISH: It's not Santa Claus, that's for sure. And I haven't seen the sheila since Monday, I'll be getting wet dreams soon.
LARRY: Saturday is the most important game of your life, Irish, and all you can do is stand there and belly-ache about your wet dreams.

IRISH: It's so bloody boring. Push, pull your head out, run about till you find another heap of fellas, find a hole to stick your head in where it's dark, push again, pull it out, run along to the next heap. You won't believe this, but at home intelligent conversation at the bottom of a ruck was not unknown. Over here, no-one talks, all you hear is grunts, growls, belches, the odd fart, and occasional snapping noises which might be teeth clamping or bones breaking, I mean you wouldn't know, it's so bloody dark you wouldn't know you'd died till the bloody whistle blew. My idea of purgatory is doing endless ruck and runs with Tupper screaming encouragement.
MEAN: It's got to be done if you want to win.
IRISH: Win? Who's going to give a tinker's whether we win or lose on Saturday, eh?
MEAN: Tupper, for one.
IRISH: Well, that's his problem. The only one here with the right attitude is Foreskin, he doesn't give a thruppenny stuff. He's got style, that lad. Did I tell you about last Saturday night after that do at Grubby's? There we were, caught red-handed, high as kites, right out of our chooks, going down a one-way street the wrong way. Next minute a siren goes, a police car pulls us over, and this traffic officer character walks up to us — big, fat fella he was. Well, Foreskin winds down his window blithe as you like, not a worry in the world, having stubbed out a roach he was drawing on not a second before. This officer fella leans down to the window and asks Foreskin, 'Did you not see the arrows, son?' 'Arrows, officer?' says Foreskin, 'I didn't even see the Indians!' Now, it may or may not be original, but that's timing, that's class.
MEAN: Yeah. But you couldn't have a team of fifteen Foreskins. It wouldn't be rugby.
IRISH: It wouldn't be barmitzvah, either.

(Mean looks vacantly at Irish.)

MEAN: Come on, Irish. With any luck we'll be cold enough to pull a muscle.

IRISH: I know one muscle that'll need pulling if this goes on much longer.

IRISH and MEAN exit through unmarked door.

LARRY: Turn over on your front laddie.

KEN turns over so that he's lying on his front facing the audience. LARRY lays his hand on KEN's thigh.

Does that hurt?

KEN: A bit.
LARRY: And further up? Here?
KEN: A bit, yes. I'm sure it's a hammy Larry, I said that.
LARRY: Yes, well now, let's just get to work on it.
KEN: I thought it wasn't wise to massage a pulled muscle.
LARRY: Tupper ordered a massage, and it's a massage you will get, my lad. You can always tell me if I'm rubbing too hard. Now just raise the tum a bit, and I'll slip down the shorts.
KEN: Is that really necessary?
LARRY: You ought to know where your hamstring runs from. No use working on the half of it, is there? You get them off lad, and I'll get the liniment.

LARRY moves to the back of the room to rustle around in a sports bag on the form.

Hope it's not serious Ken.

He returns to the table with a large bottle of liniment.

Now look at those shorts, I can't leave you to do anything by yourself, can I?

LARRY carefully pulls KEN's shorts down, and begins to massage KEN's leg with slow, gentle strokes.

ACT 1

There now lad, that's better isn't it? You've really been in the wars lately, haven't you? No sooner over the concussion than the hamstring goes. Never rains but it pours.

KEN: Doesn't seem to be too bad.
LARRY: You'll be right as rain for Saturday.

Pause

KEN: Larry, do you know anything about heads — concussion like?
LARRY: Well, I doubt that there's a great deal to be known about it really — a bang on the bonker is a bang on the old bonker — plain bad luck. Now don't you worry, I've warmed the whole thing up. Can you feel back with your hand and show me the exact spot where you felt the twinge?

KEN raises himself on the bench, begins to reach back with one hand, hesitates, then flops down again.

LARRY: Did it go again just then?
KEN: No, it never went at all.
LARRY: What's that now Ken?
KEN: I said it's not the hamstring. There's nothing wrong with the leg Larry. I'm sorry.

KEN sits up on the bench to face LARRY.

LARRY: Not the leg? I don't understand.
KEN: I got dizzy and fell over. All of a sudden. I was okay as soon as I hit the ground. Felt like a real girl.
LARRY: Oh.
KEN: I didn't feel well before that either, as soon as I began to run around. Maybe I shouldn't be running around. The doctor at the hospital said not to even train for a while.
LARRY: I suppose you've got to expect a few after-effects. I remember someone saying that it was like a bad hangover.
KEN: No hangover I've had lasted five days.

LARRY: You'll be right as rain by Saturday. It's a big game for us Ken. Most important of the season, traditionally. You'll enjoy it once you're out there.
KEN: Maybe I won't be out there.
LARRY: That's no way for a captain to speak Ken.
KEN: I'm not playing well anyway.
LARRY: That's just the point. You've got to play. I'd hate to see you lose the captaincy.

Pause

KEN: The captaincy? It'll be the first game I've missed all season.
LARRY: You're not in an easy position. I know the lads Ken, I listen to what's going on. Just between you and me, as friends, if you want to stay captain then you'd better play, all team considerations aside.
KEN: What is all this Larry?
LARRY: Maybe I've said too much already.
KEN: Come on Larry, what's going on.
LARRY: You realise that Tupper is the kind of coach who likes the captain to be a forward, a leader who's more involved, a leader by example?
KEN: I have gathered that, yes.
LARRY: Well, now that Clean's back . . . I mean he's already captain of the forwards. I'm sure he wants to be team captain.
KEN: I'm sure he does.
LARRY: Clean's not like the others Kenny. He's ambitious, ambitious to a fault. Besides, he's not a sensitive fellow like yourself.
KEN: Jesus Larry. If he wants it that much, he can have it.
LARRY: Now, now, lad, that's no attitude. As captain you've a lot of responsibilities, but a win on Saturday against Ngapuk would mean a great deal to the lads Ken. I mean, in many ways it's not been an outstanding season, but a win on Saturday would bring it right with a bang. Things would lift, and we'll have the party to end all parties at my place on Saturday night. And you'll suddenly be the captain of a real team, all right behind you.
KEN: You're the only person who's ever had a party for this team and invited them back a second time.

LARRY: Oh, they're not so bad.
KEN: They damn near wrecked your house last time Larry.
LARRY: Oh well, that's life you know. They're such a nice bunch of lads, really, like a big rowdy family. I think it's occasions like those that cement the team together, build team spirit. I like to be a part of it, I've no family or anything, not here anyway.
KEN: Wasn't that your daughter you had staying with you over the summer?
LARRY: Oh yes, with two little tykes of her own.
KEN: Then you had a wife once?

Pause

Perhaps I shouldn't be asking.

LARRY: Oh that's all right, just the usual, everyone's so blasé about it these days. We weren't ... compatible, as they say. Seemed like the thing to do at the time, marriage, you know. I had no idea what a woman was, if the truth be known, how ... demanding. Sounds silly in this day and age, doesn't it? You lads wouldn't be making that sort of mistake.

LARRY *continues rubbing* KEN'S *leg, as if in a dream. Silence, broken by sounds of the team getting closer outside.* TUPPER *storms in, out of breath, furious. He's wearing grey trousers (or baggy rugby shorts) with the bottoms tucked into yellow and black striped football socks and old-style high ankle rugby boots. His paunch is barely restrained by a rugby jersey or a heavy woollen freezing works jersey; he has a whistle hanging around his neck on the end of a boot-lace and he's carrying a muddy ball.*
TUPPER *looks at* LARRY *and* KEN. *He seems temporarily at a loss for words, or breath, then charges to the door again, bellowing.*

TUPPER: Jesus fucken wept! That was pathetic. You bastards are so slow you couldn't pull a sailor off your sister! Get excited about it! Whaddarya?
FORESKIN: Now that's an interesting philosophical question.

TUPPER *charges out the door again in response.*

TUPPER: Foreskin, keep your mouth shut. Just concentrate on the play, or I'll be pulling your tit for a change. Now listen lads, I don't want anything clever —
FORESKIN: No fear of that Tupper.
TUPPER: Foreskin I'm warning you. I won't be held responsible, son.
FORESKIN: Sorry Dad.
TUPPER: Don't call me Dad. I'd be ashamed to have a long-haired git like you for a son.
FORESKIN: Talented though, Tupper, talented.
TUPPER: Oh f'chrissakes. Will you shut your mouth or will I have to stick my size thirteen down it?

TUPPER *leans against the door wearily.*

KEN: Don't say anything Larry.
LARRY: Course not lad.
TUPPER: Right, now where was I?
FORESKIN: We were doing something clever. Must have been an accident. Then you said —

TUPPER *charges out again.*

TUPPER: I know what I fucken said. We've got to concentrate on the basics right? Kick shit out of everything, right? Okay, now let's see . . . oh, that'll about do.

TUPPER *blows a whistle.*

All right, a couple of fast circuits to finish with, but Clean, Mean, Irish, Foreskin, I want to have a chat with you senior guys in the old dressing shed before you go, no nipping off home after the shower for you. Right, what are the rest of you waiting for? Get going! Two circuits I said.
FORESKIN: Who brought the cornflakes?

Pause. TUPPER *re-enters.*

ACT 1

TUPPER: Kenny lad, you're looking 100 per cent already. Those magic fingers done the trick Larry?
LARRY: You'll have to ask the lad.
TUPPER: Well skipper? Are you or aren't you?
KEN: Skipper?
TUPPER: Ready, lad, ready to go.
KEN: Don't know Tupper.
TUPPER: That wasn't the answer I wanted to hear Ken.
KEN: I'm sorry Tee, it's the truth.
TUPPER: Gorn it's all in the mind.
KEN: That's what I'm afraid of.
TUPPER: In a sec the boys will be back in to hear about the team for Saturday. You'll be the skipper of that team Ken, because if you're not, you might never be again. It's hard, but we can't afford to fuck about at this stage. All this shilly-shallying around is bad for the team's morale.

Pause

KEN: Then I guess I play.
TUPPER: Good on you Ken. Take old Clean, six weeks back he was KOed for three hours, twenty-five stitches in his head, lost half his ear, and he was back training on the Tuesday, and played with the stitches in on the Saturday. Had to be restitched again that night, but the team won, understand? Jesus, if we had fifteen like him we could take on the whole Taranaki team and come out on top.
KEN: From what I hear Clean's sister already has.
TUPPER: Let's leave Clean's sister out of this!

Pause

TUPPER: Look son, you're captain of this team, but you're not playing like a captain, not the example you should be to the rest of the team. But here's your big chance, don't you see? KOed out of your scone last week, hero this week! This is the stuff of rugby, this is how legends are made!

KEN: And bodies broken. The doctor told me not to even train for a month.
TUPPER: Let me be the judge of that. These bloody quacks have never even played the game! You won't get hurt son, I guarantee you.
KEN: Well, okay Tupper. But I wish you'd put it in writing so I could show Cathy.
TUPPER: Your wife? Whaddarya?

> IRISH, MEAN, FORESKIN and CLEAN enter through the unmarked door, all in muddy rugby gear. As the others make their way to their bags and clothes, talking, some looking for cigarettes, CLEAN approaches the massage table where KEN is still sitting with his legs up on the table.

CLEAN: Well, that's a nice change Ken. Greasy leg instead of greasy palm.

> *Clean winks obviously.*

KEN: What the hell are you on about now Clean?
CLEAN: Greasy palm. That's the way it goes in the high finance building contracting business, isn't it? All rake-offs, kick-backs, under the table deals, a little more sand in the concrete, eh?
KEN: Come off it Clean. You've been reading too many *Time* magazines.
CLEAN: There, there, you just relax, don't let it worry you Kenny boy.

> CLEAN approaches KEN and begins to rub his hands up KEN'S leg as LARRY pulls away. KEN gets off the table abruptly and IRISH comes up behind CLEAN and begins caressing CLEAN'S chest, seductively rolling up CLEAN'S jersey. CLEAN faces LARRY across the massage table, moaning and writhing in ecstacy. IRISH gradually begins to slip CLEAN'S shorts down. The others, who have begun to change out of their rugby gear, stop and watch the performance, until CLEAN is nude except for dirty jockstrap, boots and socks. CLEAN bends forward

over the massage table and IRISH *pretends to enter him from behind. They writhe to orgasm, then leap back from the table together, joining arms at the shoulder like Greek dancers, still facing* LARRY, *who is somewhat trapped behind the table.* LARRY *copes with* CLEAN'S *performance by trying to smile and by fussing about with bottles of liniment and rolls of plaster.* CLEAN *and* IRISH *begin singing as they dance.*

CLEAN AND IRISH: Oh, we are the boys from down on the farm, we really know our cheese.

Both dip their shorts/jock-strap to expose their penises to LARRY.

CLEAN: There's much better value in turdale,
IRISH: It never fails to please.
CLEAN: Turdale comes so thickly.
IRISH: There's no waste.

As they sing this last line, both affect limp-wristed caricatures of homosexuals.

CLEAN AND IRISH: And boy it's got a mighty taste!

CLEAN *and* IRISH *laugh heartily.* LARRY *tries to smile and withdraw to his carry-all, but* CLEAN *calls to him.*

CLEAN: Hey, Larry, seriously, I think I've pulled my achilles here or something. Would you mind having a look?

CLEAN *turns his back towards* LARRY, *and looks down at his ankle.* LARRY *hesitates for a moment, then, pleased to be useful, approaches* CLEAN *like an eager puppy.* CLEAN *positions himself so that* LARRY'S *face is almost against* CLEAN'S *buttocks as he examines the ankle.*

TUPPER: What's the trouble Clean?
CLEAN: Well, Tupper, it's not that it's really bad . . .

He farts loudly, virtually in LARRY's *face.*

but it's sure as hell rotten!

General laughter, FORESKIN *being a notable exception.*

FORESKIN: For chrissakes leave the guy alone will you. It's no skin off your nose what he is or isn't.

CLEAN: It's not the skin off my nose I'd be worried about, Foreskin.

Laughter

C'mon Foreskin, just kidding, you know me. Some of us never got the benefit of a univarsity education.

Some laughter, but mainly silence as FORESKIN *eyes* CLEAN.

FORESKIN: Some of us would need a lot more help than that.

CLEAN: Watch — (your fucken)

TUPPER: Come on you bastards, the quicker we're showered and dressed the quicker we can get our little talk over and go home.

The players continue changing out of their rugby gear during the following dialogue, then grabbing their towels and getting ready to exit through the door marked 'shower'.

As MEAN *steps out of his shorts, he holds them up for inspection.*

MEAN: Look at that, me last pair. How Pat's going to get these clean for Saturday I don't know.

TUPPER: Buy yourself a spare pair.

MEAN: I used to have four pairs, but that Irish bastard keeps ripping them. First scrum every Saturday, sure enough, I'm running to the next ruck with me strides round me ankles. What have you got against me strides Irish?

IRISH: Nothing. But it sure as hell tickles me fancy to see you baring your pimply backside in front of the grand-stand every week.

MEAN: Well cut it out, the wife thinks I'm going kinky.

IRISH: Be warned, Mean me lad. This Saturday your jock-strap goes too. Ping!

MEAN: Right, that does it. I'm going to eat three square meals of baked beans, onions, and boiled eggs on Friday. Come Saturday, you won't be able to get your nose within a yard of my arse.

IRISH: That's all right, I never liked scrums anyway.

TUPPER: That's been quite obvious all season. A No. 8 is meant to push, not lean.

IRISH: Well, if Mean's tanked up on onions, beans and eggs, there's no way I'm sticking my delicate olfactory appendage between his legs.

MEAN: You're not going to have any strength left for ripping shorts, that's for sure. Cost a bloody fortune.

CLEAN: Yeah, go easy on poor old Mean. He might have to sell half his farm, then he'd only own a quarter of the bloody province.

MEAN: You bloody townies have got no idea.

FORESKIN: Come on Meanie, tell us some more of those agricultural riddles. Like how to tell the difference between wet and dry ewes. It's not just the wether, is it?

MEAN: You'd learn the difference pretty quick if you were a lamb sucking on a dry tit!

Overplayed stunned reaction by the team.

EVERYONE: Oooh, Meanie!

IRISH goes across to MEAN during the following speech, puts his hand on MEAN'S shoulder, and speaks to him in a loud aside, for the team's benefit.

IRISH: That sounds a bit pornographic — sure you're not a bit, you know, well, has a sheep ever started looking a bit, you know, attractive — ever caught yourself thinking, well, what a lovely set of, ah, shanks?

Everyone laughs, much to MEAN'S discomfort.

MEAN: Now hold on there Irish — a man can take a joke as good as the rest, but crikey dick, that's a bit — (on the nose)

FORESKIN: What about you Tupper? They must know about these things in Taranaki, surely — or would you say they were more into cows there?
TUPPER: I'll give you Taranaki round the ear, you cheeky young bugger. Taranaki would have straightened you out all right.
FORESKIN: Gorn, Tupper, I bet you were as bent as a hairpin in your far-off forgotten youth.
TUPPER: It's not bloody forgotten. Or far-off. I've had a bloody hard life, that's all. Fight a bloody world war and what do you get?
FORESKIN: The only thing that worried you Tee, was where your next square meal was coming from.
TUPPER: Ten years from now you'll be laughing on the other side of your face, you whippersnapper.
FORESKIN: Tell us about '56, Tupper, that'll bring the flush of youth back to you. What really happened between Bekker and Skinner?
TUPPER: Well, it's funny you should mention farting, that was the root of the whole problem. These bloody Afrikaaners have a funny diet, you know, Bantu, Hottentots, the odd Indian or Cape Coloured for dessert, and the smell — oooh!

At this point the players begin throwing discarded gear at TUPPER, *who retreats naked and laughing through the door marked 'shower'.* IRISH, CLEAN, MEAN, *also naked, pursue him with towels. Left on stage still changing are* FORESKIN *and* KEN, *with* LARRY *sitting disconsolately in a corner.*

FORESKIN: Don't let it get to you Larry. They're scared of what they don't understand, that's all.
LARRY: Oh no worries lad, no worries.

Pause

FORESKIN: Well, what do you think for Saturday Kenny? From the point of view of an impartial observer, well, observer anyway.
KEN: Seems I'm not going to be on the sideline after all Seymour.
FORESKIN: Jesus Kenny, you're not thinking of playing?
KEN: Seems as if I am.

FORESKIN: You've got to be out of your head! Listen, even two-bit pugs who fight for blood and money have to take a compulsory three month holiday after they're KOed.
KEN: That's different Seymour, they're pros. As Tupper says, maybe it's time I earned my stripes as skipper and set an example.
FORESKIN: What kind of example?
KEN: Clean got worse a while back, and he played on.
FORESKIN: That's different mate, and you know it. You've got Catherine and the kids to think of, the contracting business. No-one is going to run it if you're not there. Jesus, you've got the whole world to think of, not just one lousy game or one lousy team. Besides, for Clean this is the world. You take away the rugby and you take away his friends, his interests, his culture — christ, I bet he doesn't even read newspapers in the off-season. Twenty or thirty years from now he'll just be a big, fat, dumb heavy, living on delusions of former glory and free beers from fans with long memories who feel sorry for him, and looking for immortality in the dregs of every glass. That's not where you're at Ken.
KEN: Thanks Seymour.

Pause

FORESKIN: What's Catherine think of all this? Does she know you're playing?
KEN: I guess not, we haven't discussed it.
FORESKIN: Well?
KEN: Well, christ Seymour, you know as well as I do that she doesn't like me playing even when I am fit. She hates the game.
FORESKIN: Bloody right she is too.
KEN: Why the hell do you play then?
FORESKIN: A man's got to have a folly. Seriously me old son, to make poetry through motion. As I've often said before, I'm a class removed from you donkeys — the laws of gravity, kinetics, time, space and kicks in the head don't apply to the likes of me.
KEN: You're a weird bastard sometimes Seymour. A good bastard but weird, you know.

Foreskin mimics Irish.

FORESKIN: How could I know, being only meself? Don't try and get me off the point. What about it?
KEN: What about what?
FORESKIN: It's decided then, you're not playing.
KEN: Ask Tupper Seymour, ask Tupper. He guarantees I'll be okay.

Pause

Listen Seymour, I feel obliged to the team.

KEN *exits.* FORESKIN *continues changing. Then, from the shower off-stage, in a loud sing-song voice:*

IRISH: Here's to the girl that I love best!
CLEAN: I love her best when she's undressed!
IRISH: I'd fuck her sitting standing lying.
CLEAN: Why, I'd even fuck her as she lay dying.
IRISH: And when she's dead and long forgotten . . .
CLEAN: I'll dig her up and fuck her rotten.

In the corner LARRY *puts his head in his hands.*

LARRY: Oh shit.
FORESKIN: I wouldn't argue.
LARRY: Why do you come back here to play Seymour? You could do much better playing for the university.

Pause

FORESKIN: It's a question of contrast, Larry. You know, sometimes up there I get the feeling life itself is just an abstraction. I like coming back here a couple of times a week, keeping some involvement. Oh, I know I couldn't live here again, but jesus Larry, you've no idea what it's like up there in the ivory tower.
LARRY: I think I know what you mean.
FORESKIN: Then you're probably way ahead of me.

ACT 1

Foreskin turns to get his towel. Larry sighs.

Bit down in the mouth Larry?

LARRY: Oh, it's nothing. Bit of pressure at work lately.
FORESKIN: Oh?

Larry gets up, puts his hands in his pockets.

LARRY: Yes, they depend on me you know. Bit much sometimes, I feel. The district manager was down last week — oh, he's a nice enough fellow, but it's a strain putting it on for them all the time. You know, away from home for a couple of days once in a blue moon, they always want to get up to a bit of mischief, no matter what age or how happily married. So, most of the time we end up absolutely sodden in some corner bar while he extolls his wife's virtues and compares all the floozies going past with the one he had in Italy during the war.
FORESKIN: Human nature Lawrence. Perhaps the wrong part is the way society makes little prisons for us to begin with — marriage, home, family, job.

Larry sits down again.

LARRY: I know someone who'd give anything for his very own prison.

Pause

FORESKIN: Yes. Well, I'd better get into the shower or those bastards will have used all the hot water. Can't stand cold showers.

Foreskin moves towards the shower door with his towel. Larry suddenly stands and goes to stop him.

LARRY: Seymour. There is something. I know it's probably not the right time . . . did you see what happened to Ken?
FORESKIN: No. Got caught in a ruck didn't he? Those donkeys

wouldn't know where they're putting their feet. No control, you know, brain . . . nervous system . . . foot . . . put.

FORESKIN *acts like an automaton as he points to his head, down to his foot, lifts it, puts it down, and claps himself as he succeeds.*

LARRY: I'm not sure . . . that it was an accident.
FORESKIN: What?
LARRY: Well, I . . . saw the boot. Clean's.
FORESKIN: You're sure?
LARRY: The boot, yes. Maybe just an accident, I mean . . .

Pause

FORESKIN: Maybe. Have you put it to him?
LARRY: No!
FORESKIN: You must. Let me know his reaction.

FORESKIN *exits to shower. Pause. Then* CLEAN *and* IRISH *enter from the shower, naked.* CLEAN *is towelling himself in a flaunting manner, singing a ditty called 'The gash that never heals'.* IRISH *sits down on the form by his clothes and begins fiddling with his transistor, trying to get the trots, during the ensuing.* LARRY *appears agitated, looks back at the shower door and then tries to take* CLEAN *by the arm and draw him downstage away from* IRISH.

LARRY: Ah, Lindsay, before the others come back, could we have a little chat, ah, man to man.

CLEAN *pulls his arm away and sits down on a form to towel his feet assiduously.*

CLEAN: Man to what?
LARRY: Oh. Well, I wouldn't have bothered you unless I felt it was important.

CLEAN *stops towelling himself, and looks up at* LARRY.

Well, ah, it's Ken. His head.

CLEAN: His problem.
LARRY: Yes. That is, yes, it would be, if. . .
CLEAN: What the fuck are you on about?
LARRY: I. . . saw what happened, that's all.

CLEAN suddenly stands up, over LARRY, threateningly.

CLEAN: Look, I don't know what you think you saw, but don't you come blabbing to me or anyone else.
LARRY: This is rugby you're using. Not just a game, a tradition — (going back)
CLEAN: Tradition! All those old warthogs crying into their beer?
LARRY: It's not worth it Clean, nothing's worth that.

CLEAN jabs LARRY in the chest.

CLEAN: Don't you try to tell me what's worth a damn and what isn't. We're not in a cotton-wool world now. I've got a wife and child to pull through the world, and that kid is not going to be sitting in a class of no-hopers getting the sort of shit thrown at him that I got. Twenty years from now, this is one cunt who won't be crying into his beer.

TUPPER, KEN and MEAN, talking amongst themselves, enter from the shower and begin dressing, having dried themselves in the shower room. LARRY and CLEAN lower their voices.

LARRY: I wonder why I bother.
CLEAN: Short answer Larry: don't.

IRISH turns up the transistor and the sound of a trotting commentary is heard. IRISH and MEAN appear to have money on the race and react accordingly. LARRY collects himself and rustles around in his bag.

Eventually he comes out with a notebook and a pen. Throughout the ensuing dialogue the players continue drying themselves and getting dressed. By the time TUPPER *intervenes everyone is changed.*

LARRY: Listen lads, how about a flutter, a sweepstake on the big game Saturday night — better still, we could celebrate victory over Ngapuk with a party at my place, and we could all stay and watch the All Blacks and the Springboks on the colour TV after, and dish out the winnings from the sweepstake — how would that be?

FORESKIN *enters from shower half way through* LARRY'S *discourse.*

FORESKIN: Immoral.
LARRY: A little flutter?
KEN: He means the apartheid thing.
CLEAN: Haven't you heard up at the univarsity? Keep politics out of sport.
FORESKIN: Oh yeah Clean, sure. And we'll keep politics off television and out of economics and taxes, and away from sex and drugs and rock'n'roll, and out of parliament and life.

FORESKIN *jumps up on the table and begins soapbox oratory, gesticulating grandly.*

And keep it off street corners, and out of rubbish tins, and away from mental defectives, minors, majors, little corporals and air commodores.

Pause. Cocks an ear. Then in cultured tones.

What's that I hear you say, madam? Some of your best friends are Maoris? And dogs, madam, dings dallies dutchies dagoes boongs chinks gooks wogs commies coconuts coons kaffirs pommies polys woollys gollys spics spucs spades spastics the PYM queers and other long-haired fairies — yes! We love them all!

There's a short silence.

MEAN: I'll take two Larry.
IRISH: Me too Larry, I'll be in on it.
LARRY: Righto lads, now what'll it be?
MEAN: Well, it's the first test and the Boks traditionally win the first one, so logic says 13-9 to the Springboks, and loyalty says, ah, let's say 10-6 to the All Blacks. How's that?
LARRY: Pretty shrewd, I'd say, Mean. What about you Irish.
IRISH: Let's not bugger about Larry — 20 to nil to the All Blacks, christ, someone's got to show a little confidence in the poor buggers.
LARRY: Come on Fore, what about you?
FORESKIN: I'll have nothing to do with it.
CLEAN: Whaddayamean? You'll watch the bloody game on television, though.
FORESKIN: I won't.
CLEAN: That's dumb. Who's going to know? Who's going to care?
FORESKIN: I'm not measuring my protest by its effect — the principle's enough at this stage.
CLEAN: You're out of your bloody tree.
FORESKIN: Hope so, but let's just leave it.
IRISH: Anyway, what about this country's great exploited majority? You make them live in depressed areas with no amenities, you spend not a penny on their education, and anything you spend on their health is just so you can exploit them the more. They outnumber you about twenty times over, but not one of them gets the vote — in fact, they're so cruelly exploited there's probably not a one of them reached voting age.
CLEAN: Gorn Irish, we haven't got jungles big enough to hide that many boongs.
IRISH: Sheep don't live in jungles.
CLEAN: Well, they do have woolly heads.
FORESKIN: Jesus!
IRISH: Come on Foreskin, don't get your jock-strap in a knot. Your average rooster doesn't give a thruppenny tinker's about any of that.

FORESKIN: Then what does he care about?
IRISH: Well, your average rooster just wants to know where his next square meal's coming from, then, where his next beer's coming from. When he can afford to be really intellectual, he starts worrying about the mortgage, and the missus, and his next naughty on the side. You see, the truth of the matter is, he's got his hands so fucken deep in his pockets holding on to his pennies, it's a wonder he hasn't had to learn to piss no hands.
LARRY: Good one Irish, don't think I'll bother going to Ireland if that's the case.
IRISH: I was talking about God's Own. In Ireland we have real problems, thank God.

TUPPER is first changed, and has taken up a position centrestage, standing directly behind the massage table. From there he has been listening incredulously and a little impatiently. By the time IRISH finishes talking everyone is more or less dressed. On the table in front of TUPPER is a large, dirty rugby boot.

TUPPER: What a load of fucken codswallop. Now lads, a little bit of hush, all right? I want a bit of concentration just for ten minutes, if that's at all possible.

He pauses, and the sound of a race commentary is clearly heard.

TUPPER: Irish, son, you're trying my patience.
IRISH: Shush, just a sec big Tee, I've got a couple of bob on the 8.50 at —
TUPPER: You turn that fucken thing off this very second son, or I won't be responsible for what follows! Understand?
IRISH: Sure, Tee, sorry about that.

IRISH turns off the transistor, making a pained aside as he does so.

IRISH: Bejesus, and they were only three furlongs out. What ails the man?

Pause. The players carry on chatting and putting their gear in their bags as TUPPER *stands centrestage.*

TUPPER: I'm a worried man!

Silence. TUPPER *acts out his conception of a worried man, head down, inhaling deeply, rubbing and pulling his several chins with one hand. Finally he stares up at the ceiling, then picks up the large boot off the table in front of him with the air of a man finally arrived at a solution.*

Now, take a good long look at this!

TUPPER *flourishes the boot, then dangles it by the laces in front of each player as he stalks about.*

It's a boot, a big, heavy, dirty boot. Now, what's it for, eh? What's it for?

IRISH: How many guesses we got?

TUPPER: It is not for keeping your feet dry in the puddles. If it was, why's it got this hard bit at one end, eh? No, no, no, no, no! It's hard at one end so you can kick things and not hurt your big toe.

IRISH: Like the ball, you'd be saying.

TUPPER: Certainly the ball, certainly the ball. But if, on occasion the ball has got the odd bit of hair on it, or an ear or such-like, then we'll give it the benefit of the doubt and kick shit out of it first and let the ref ask questions after. Don't be too obvious, mind, we're grown men and we know the game — a bit of ruthlessness, a bit of hate. I know most of those lads and I'm telling you a bit of the old boot in the right place at the right time and they'll throw it in. We've got to be absolutely uncompromising, sicken them in the first twenty minutes so that they don't want to play. Kick and rake anything within yards of the ball, they'll lose their appetite pretty damn quickly. This is . . . psychological.

IRISH: Psycho-what?

TUPPER: Stands to reason. Doesn't matter how brave they are, how badly they want to win, when they've had it in the swede at one ruck, they're going to be just that much slower getting to the next one.

Now, Clean, Mean, you boys are the key here. I'm not going to say too much to you individually at this point because we're still two days away from the game and I wouldn't expect you to keep it in your heads that long. But listen, Clean, I've been more impressed with you lately, much more ruthless. I don't know whether it was that kick in the head or joining the force that did it, but keep it up son.

TUPPER *pats* CLEAN *on the head appreciatively.*

Mean, you've got to show some improvement son. I'm telling you this for your own good — if you want to make the rep team this year, you'll have to get that edge. Last week I saw you step over some bod on the ground on the way to a ruck — the ref was on the other side — blind! Son, a true rep player would not have stepped over that bastard,

TUPPER *grabs a handful of* MEAN'S *hair and shakes* MEAN'S *head*

he'd have stepped on him, run through him! You're the prime example of someone who's got to get a little more hate into his game, otherwise the glories of the rep stuff will be little more than a dream.

Now Irish — Jeez, you'd be a mis-shapen looking bastard — ideal! Now, where I come from, a No. 8 is not an imitation loosie, all right? I want you to stay in the tight all day. I want you to be like those pit ponies, blind from lack of light — and not for any other reason mind. However, you will be playing off the end of the lineout. For two reasons: (a) you're as fast as my grandmother downing Guiness on payday, and secondly, you're as ugly as sin. I want you to go off the end of that lineout like a rocket, straight at their first-five. Now, I'm not expecting you to catch him every time, but if you can get within a couple of yards

of him, he'll get a good look at your ugly mug and if he's got any brains at all, he'll be scared shitless for the rest of the game and drop the ball. That's the key, ball on the ground, we know what to do with it. What do we do with it? Clean?
CLEAN: Kick shit out of it, Tupper.
TUPPER: And if they've got the ball in the hand, what do we do? Irish?
IRISH: Drop them.
TUPPER: And where will the ball be then? Mean?
MEAN: On the ground, Tupper.
TUPPER: And what do we do with it then? Everyone?
ALL: Kick shit out of everything, Tupper.
TUPPER: Righto! So that's the general strategy! We kick shit out of everything above grass height, and we keep the ball ahead of us. I know you forwards will do me proud. It's the backs I'm worried about.
  It's very simple, you backs. All you have to do is keep the ball in front of the forwards. Either the half-back has a go on his own close to the scrum and links back with the forwards, or he passes it back to you Ken, and you hoist it as high as possible, give the forwards time to get under it. I don't know what you've been playing at recently Ken. All this airy-fairy stuff, running for gaps I couldn't squeeze my doodle into. You've got to exercise more control son, wait till the gap opens up.
KEN: Tupper, it doesn't work like that. I can't wait till I see a gap you could drive a horse and dray through. It's got to be instinct. If I actually see the gap consciously before I'm into it and through it, then it's too late.
TUPPER: Okay Ken, okay. But I do want more control, less of this playing it by ear. You should be planning ahead, strategy.
KEN: Sure, but what if I plan to spin it, then get slow service, and everyone's crept up flat? What if it's a ruck in the middle, and I planned to go right, but the numbers say go left?
TUPPER: What numbers?
KEN: Their numbers as against ours. When we're mid-field, we split and they split, not often even, there's got to be more one side than the other, it all happens pretty fast. If they haven't covered

our formation properly, surely I've got to go that side, we ought to get the overlap.

TUPPER: All this bloody calculator stuff be buggered. In our day the best tactic for a five-eighth was to either pin his ears back or root it so high it had snow on it when it came down.

KEN: Yes Tupper, the point is —

TUPPER: The point is I want a lot less risks taken back there. A no-risks policy for Saturday.

FORESKIN: That's a contradiction in terms Tupper. The game is rugby, how can you eliminate risks, that's the whole point of the game.

TUPPER: The point of the bloody game, son, is to win. That's the bloody point. Clear? I don't want anything remotely clever.

FORESKIN: That possibility is certainly remote.

TUPPER: You're the worst offender Foreskin.

TUPPER *goes to* KEN *and pats him paternally on the head.*

I don't know what kind of ideas you've been putting into Kenny's head, but I don't want to see any more of this attacking with the extra man in from our own twenty-five.

FORESKIN: Twenty-two.

TUPPER: Wog measurement, whatever.

FORESKIN: Anyway, as I remember it, we scored a try from that move. What more do you want?

TUPPER: I'm not complaining about the try Foreskin, you did very well. But it's not rugby son, attacking like that, it's not pure. Any idiot can run the ball from one end to the other. It's what happens in between that's important.

IRISH: Back in the bog we have this rule that says the team that scores the most points, including tries, before the referee blows the whistle, wins the game.

TUPPER: Don't you get smart — we haven't lost to you Irish bastards yet, so don't come over here handing out the advice.

IRISH: Oh no, I wouldn't presume, honest to god. In fact I was wanting some. Seeing as how I'm playing No. 8 and all, I was

ACT 1   47

wondering whether you'd be wanting a few scintillating moves off the back of the scrum.
TUPPER: Listen Irish, one half-back is enough. You just keep your head buried. What we need is a few more ideas behind the scrum, a few crash-balls or the like.
FORESKIN: I've got a few ideas Tupper.
TUPPER: I'm not sure I want to hear them.
FORESKIN: You did ask.
TUPPER: Well go on then.
FORESKIN: This idea doesn't apply to the backs. In fact, in this team, it would probably apply more to the forwards.
TUPPER: How?
FORESKIN: The idea is called social responsibility on the field. It goes like this: every player knows every time he steps on the field that if he plays the game correctly, he's going to be flat on his back or front absolutely helpless at least twenty times during every game.
TUPPER: So. I don't follow you.
FORESKIN: Didn't think you would Tupper. So, every player who steps on to the field knows that there are going to be at least twenty opportunities for any moron on the other side to maim him for life.
TUPPER: What the hell has this got to do with anything son?
FORESKIN: Just this, Tupper. If any player knew for sure that there was such a moron in the opposition, would he step on to the field in the first place?
TUPPER: I don't see that this has got anything to do with Saturday Foreskin.
FORESKIN: No, you wouldn't, and that's the real pity of it Tupper.

FORESKIN *rises to his feet.*

When I step on to the field I accept that any two-bit moron could kick my head into little pieces, or put me in a wheelchair for life. But I believe it won't happen, of course, otherwise I wouldn't step out there, none of us would. I believe in the good intentions of my fellow players, I believe in their good fellowship, I believe that they're out there for the same good purpose that I am, I believe in their sense of responsibility towards me as another human being, I believe in their social responsibility. Now do you understand?

TUPPER: I understand, all right. I understand that you're some kind of free spirit poofter is what I understand.

FORESKIN: I think you understand that I'm talking about a coach who tells his players to go out there and be two-bit morons.

Pause. TUPPER'S *head drops for a second or two, then he looks up.*

TUPPER: Son, I've believed in your talent as a footballer since you were very young — you always had far more pure ability than any five of the other kids. That's why it's specially sad to see that talent abused. You could have gone a long way in the game. You seem to insist on trying to fuck it up for everyone else. This is a team game, son, and the town is the team. It's the town's honour at stake when the team plays, god knows there's not much else around here. Now, you've been away to the univarsity and had some funny ideas put into your head, some funny ideas you've got to get rid of if you want to keep playing here. It's not just your little speech here tonight either. Last Friday night, for instance, you were seen getting back with some floozy at all hours, and that's not the first time. Since you're so keen on responsibility, perhaps you'd like to explain that to your team-mates.

FORESKIN: All right. Every Thursday night when I listen to your team-talk, Tupper, I get worried. I begin thinking about some of the horrible things they could do to me. Then I have trouble getting off to sleep, and when I do, I have this nightmare — every other night of the week I dream about blondes, but on Thursday nights, sure as hell, I'm standing under my goal-posts waiting for an up-and-under to come down — and the whole Canterbury pack ten yards away and closing fast. I wait there for an eternity, willing that ball to drop faster so I can catch it and clear it before the pack arrives, but deep inside I know that the pack and the ball are going to arrive simult . . . at the same time. Then I start willing the ball to go back up, but it comes on just the same, and just as the crunch comes I brace myself — and wake up sweating in a heap on the floor clutching my cock for dear life because I think I've lost it on the end of someone's sprigs! So I hold on to my cock for the rest of the night and fret about all the beautiful blondes I'll never have. Then I start thinking, damn it, if this is the last night we're together, then I'm going to make the most of it, I'm going to have one last lovely lady to remember it by.

Pause. FORESKIN *looks at an incredulous* TUPPER. *Some of the other players are sniggering.*

TUPPER: Well that takes the fucken cake! I have never heard such a rank, bullshit excuse in all my born days!

FORESKIN: I sleep like a baby, honest. I like ladies.

TUPPER: Well, you're young son, you'll get over it. In a couple of years' time you'll rather have a glass of beer any day. Unfortunately, when that day arrives you'll be bugger all good for rugby either. We can't wait. Can't you see you're letting the team down tiring yourself out like that? You can do all the fucking you like on Saturday night after the game is over — if we've won son, you'll be a hero and you'll have the pick of the girls.

IRISH: He does even when we lose.

FORESKIN: Tupper, you're living in the stone age. Women don't give a fuck about rugby players — why should they? All they ever talk about is side-steps, hooks against the head and working the blind-side. By the time they get into the pit they're too shikkered and tired and knocked up to even think about giving someone else a bit of pleasure.

TUPPER: Enough of this fucken heresy Foreskin! Play the game. I'm telling you straight that any more of this Friday night carry-on and you'll be out on your arse.

FORESKIN: Well, if it's got to be. . . .

TUPPER: You don't seem to realise son, nothing's got to be. It's all up to you. Play the fucken game.

> FORESKIN *shrugs. Silence.* TUPPER *seems distracted. He picks up the boot again and begins to flourish it, then with an exasperated air he puts it down again.*

> I s'pose we can leave it there. Time's getting on. Gorn, off you go, you buggers. Let's see you raring to go come Saturday, give the others a lead.

> *Players begin rising, picking up bags.* LARRY *jumps to his feet.*

LARRY: Just one thing. A little reminder — party after the game for everyone at my place. Then we can watch the big game on the telly.
CLEAN: That include the Ngapuk jokers?
LARRY: Certainly it does.
CLEAN: And the fluff?
LARRY: Oh yes, wives and girl-friends too, I think. Unless you'd rather . . .
KEN: The Ngapuk lads usually bring their ladies.
CLEAN: Fluff it is then.

> *Players begin leaving, calling goodbyes, arranging lifts.* TUPPER *approaches* FORESKIN *who is standing and obviously about to go.*

TUPPER: Would you mind staying on a bit after the others, Foreskin? Maybe we should have a bit of a yarn.

> FORESKIN *nods and sits down.* TUPPER *leans wearily on the door frame and waves to the departing players to the sound of cars starting and fading into the distance.* TUPPER *turns back to* FORESKIN *and slowly begins packing his gear into his bag.*

> You shouldn't have done that to me, not in front of the troops.

> *Pause*

> It's very discouraging. A team-talk shouldn't go like that.

FORESKIN: I agree.

Pause

TUPPER: I'm no ogre Seymour. A coach has got to take a stance in front of the team. You realise that, surely. It's expected.

Pause

A lot of what I do in front of the team is just . . . acting. A coach must be a bit of an actor — for psychological reasons. Like my bawling you out. I didn't like doing that, but you were threatening the team. Can you understand that?

FORESKIN: Who is the team Tupper? What is the team? There's just a collection of human beings. The team has no magical properties of its own.

TUPPER: That's where we disagree. The highest, best thing that most of these lads will experience in their lives — the finest thing I've ever experienced — is that sense of comradeship, striving for the common goal, all together, one! That's it for me. That *was* it.

FORESKIN: Everyone has their dope Tupper. I'm not disagreeing with anything you've said —

TUPPER: You're too much of an individual. You're a bloody romantic!

FORESKIN: How can that be a disqualification?

TUPPER: I'll try to explain. You're an individual with a lot of skill. But that's not it, that's not the truth about rugby. It's always been a test of guts and character, not skill. And it's better that way; a man, an ordinary bloke, can find out a lot about himself and his mates. I see my part as building a platform, a standard for the team to try for. And that standard has got to be one of guts, of character, of desire, of the spirit to go through the fire, the war, the dangers with your mates, and come out stronger for it at the other end. Do you understand? You must!

FORESKIN: The only thing I don't agree with is that it takes character or guts to kick another player in the head. Not when he's lying flat on his back.

TUPPER *rises, walks over to his bag.*

TUPPER: Don't take all that too seriously Seymour. That 'kick shit out of everything' act is just that, an act. I know those lads, they're not going to go out there and kick anyone, I know that. It's enough that they feel it! That it's hard, serious, important. A battle worth winning.

FORESKIN *rises, bag in hand.*

FORESKIN: How well do you think you know these people? There's fifteen individuals out there in your team. By the law of averages some of them are going to be angry, frustrated, bitter, wife beaters, rapists, or maybe just overwhelmed by the mortgage. Can you predict what they'll do when they're let loose in a provocative atmosphere for eighty minutes? That's a lot of seconds, a millenium of split-seconds to account for. Can you know them so well?

TUPPER *moves to the door backstage, stops and turns, with his hand on the latch.*

TUPPER: You make them sound like a bunch of criminals. They're not, they're just ordinary blokes, salt of the earth.
FORESKIN: That's my point Tupper. You're the romantic.

Pause

TUPPER: Come on son, want a lift home?

TUPPER *holds the door open.* FORESKIN *goes to move towards the door, then stops.*

FORESKIN: Don't make Ken play, Tupper.

ACT 1

TUPPER: Make him play? Who's making him play? It's completely up to him.
FORESKIN: He feels obliged.
TUPPER: There are obligations in life that have to be faced.
FORESKIN: His only obligation is guilt. That's why he's captain, isn't it?
TUPPER: I don't follow you. Again.
FORESKIN: He's a nice guy. Absolutely predictable. You can make him feel duty to the team and guilt whenever you want to.
TUPPER: It's a pity he has to feel that to make him want to play.
FORESKIN: You can't just confine your responsibilities like that Tupper. There's a larger game.
TUPPER: What?
FORESKIN: Life. Ken's life, for instance. For the 95% of it that he's not playing rugby.
TUPPER: That's a smaller game, life! None of the grand emotions.
FORESKIN: Jesus you'd be an incorrigible old prick.
TUPPER: And you haven't a brain in your fucken head despite all your fancy talk and university education! Still, I'm willing to forget all that and just be mates.
FORESKIN: How can we be mates? I don't agree with a word you say, with a thought in that log of wood you call your head. We don't agree on anything important.
TUPPER: Important? Important my arse. The best mates I've ever had, we never got past the time of day. What's important? You just get on with it. I've heard about you student buggers, sitting around with cups of coffee putting the world to rights, baring your lily-arsed souls. You need a good root up the khyber and told to get on with it — a wife, couple of screaming kids and mortgaged to the tonsils. It'd do wonders for your perspective of the world, you wouldn't be able to get down here fast enough of a Tuesday or Thursday night.

FORESKIN *shakes his head.*

FORESKIN: You old bull. You know something funny about you and me Tupper? Essentially we're on the same side.
TUPPER: Which side?

FORESKIN: Altruism.
TUPPER: Crap. I don't even know what it means.

> TUPPER *exits. Pause.* TUPPER *pokes his head around the door.*

TUPPER: Well. Do you want a bloody lift or don't you?

> FORESKIN *walks towards* TUPPER. TUPPER *holds the door open wider, puts a hand on* FORESKIN'S *shoulder to guide him through the doorway, and follows, switching off the light as he goes.*

INTERVAL

Act Two

Set — A verandah outside LARRY'S *house, inside which the after-match party is taking place. There are two easy chairs and a small coffee table on the verandah. There must be a progression from the familiar, rooted reality of Act One, and of* CLEAN'S *opening speech in Act Two, to increasingly dislocated, unfamiliar, self-revelatory scenes. The dislocation and self-revelation must be seen against a background of heavy drinking, which is being carried on throughout Act Two by all the characters involved.*

Noise of party in progress. FORESKIN *is standing alone on the verandah. He paces back and forth, sometimes stopping to listen to the proceedings inside, other times turning quickly away in disgust. Sometimes, during the more traditional parts of* CLEAN'S *speech, he mimes the words as* CLEAN'S *voice is heard speaking them, as if repeating a liturgy. The following can clearly be heard from off-stage.*

LARRY: Bit of hush please ladies and gentlemen.

Pause, while noise continues unabated.

Quiet, please.

Noise continues as before.

Excuse me ladies and gentlemen, a bit of hush, please.

Pause. No abatement of noise.

CLEAN: Shut up you bastards and listen.

Silence.

Righto. I know damn well you don't want to listen to me make a speech any more than I want to make it.
IRISH: Then it's unanimous — let's party.

Noise begins again.

CLEAN: Hold it, hold it. Jeez Irish, sometimes I could wring your — there are some things that have to be done.
IRISH: Why?
CLEAN: Because it's . . . customary, that's why.

IRISH *blows a raspberry.*

CLEAN: Listen fuck-face — oops, sorry ladies. Just put a sock in it for a mo, Irish, you can have your say later.
IRISH: Promise?
CLEAN: Righto. As I was saying, unaccustomed as I am — oh, sorry, better get this right. Ladies, gentlemen, Larry.

Pause for laughs.

As captain —

Interjections, boos, some mention of KEN'S *name.*

As acting captain of the Kaitaki team, and unaccustomed as I am, I'd like to welcome our visitors of the Ngapuk club here tonight. It's a real shame you couldn't bring your ladies after all — or that we had to. Joke, joke. Anyway, it's nice to get together over a beer after a tough game and have a bit of a yarn. Now, I'd like to say a few words about the game today. First off, congratulations to you Ngapuk bastards for winning it — gives us something to aim for next year. I felt most of our lads played well, gave guts, and I feel that if we'd held a few more passes — and given at least one more, where's that bloody Foreskin? — and had a bit of luck with our kicking —
IRISH: And said two hundred hail marys and offered ourselves up for divine providence and missionary positions in heathen parts —

CLEAN: — we'd have done you for a dinner, taken you to the cleaners. Still, as I say, we were edged out, and all credit to Ngapuk. I'd ask our players to be upstanding and drink a bumper toast to Ngapuk — to Ngapuk.
ALL: To Ngapuk.
CLEAN: Forrr...
ALL: They are jolly good fellows
For they are jolly good fellows
For they are jolly good fellows
And so say all of us
And so say all of us
And so say all of us.
It's the way it was in the army
The way it was in the navy
Way it is on the football field
And so say all of us.
CLEAN: Hip-
ALL: Ray.
CLEAN: Hip-
ALL: Ray.
CLEAN: Hip-
ALL: Ray.
CLEAN: Righto. Now the ref today was Jimmy Plunkett. I thought he did not a bad job, except when it came to dishing out penalties. Still, a difficult game to ref, I'd imagine, so all in all, well done Jim. One for the ref. Hip-
ALL: Ray.
CLEAN: Righto, fair enough. Now, sometimes I joke about the, ah, fairer sex, though I prefer them dark meself, ha ha, joke, joke. But really, we're glad to have you here tonight because, thanks to you ladies, we've got a great feed coming up. All the ladies brought some goodies — and a plate, too.

Laughs and cheers.

CLEAN: So let's hear it for the womenfolk and their plates. Hip-
ALL: Ray.

CLEAN: Righto. One last call going out to Larry. Thanks for the use of your pad, Larry. You may be a bit of a poof, but you're okay — at a distance of more than six inches, ha ha. Right, thanks for listening, let's get back to some serious boozing. Better still, what about a boat-race? Give us a chance for revenge, youse Ngapuk bastards.

General noise resumes, punctuated by frequent calls of 'Blow your froth', 'Drink', and 'Redrink'. There's also lots of banging of glasses and the occasional breaking of same and of bottles — these sounds should form a background for some minutes during the following dialogue, at least until CLEAN'S *entrance on to the verandah. At present,* FORESKIN *is still alone on the verandah, head bowed, as* MOIRA *joins him.*

MOIRA: So this is where you're hiding. What on earth are you doing out here?
FORESKIN: Mourning.
MOIRA: Who for?
FORESKIN: A rugby player I used to know.
MOIRA: Ken? Bit premature isn't it?
FORESKIN: Not necessarily. This player might not be playing the game again.
MOIRA: No great loss.
FORESKIN: Oh, but it is.
MOIRA: And Ken?
FORESKIN: Unconscious.
MOIRA: Still?
FORESKIN: The hospital keeps saying, 'It's too early to tell.'
MOIRA: To tell what?
FORESKIN: They won't elaborate.

Pause. MOIRA *lights a cigarette. There is a burst of noise as* LARRY *enters.*

MOIRA: Hello, another refugee.
LARRY: More like exile.

ACT 2   59

MOIRA: You seem rather sanguine about it all Larry.
LARRY: You get used to it.
MOIRA: It's such a lovely place, why don't you get angry, leap about?
LARRY: It'd only increase the violence. Particularly to me.
MOIRA: They're a lot of pigs. Why do they drink like that?
LARRY: I don't know. Fills a hole, they say.
MOIRA: The void.
LARRY: Pardon?
MOIRA: Void. That's bigger than a hole.
LARRY: I imagine so.
FORESKIN: Deep.
MOIRA: I enjoy weak puns, don't you Larry?
LARRY: Ah . . .
MOIRA: You know what the real trouble is?
LARRY: No idea probably.
MOIRA: Well, we're brought up to believe that we don't need an attitude towards booze — or towards work, sex, our old people, or babies. We have this incredible cocoon of rules, regulations, licensing, benefits, which supposedly makes a moral attitude superfluous — unnecessary, you understand?
LARRY: Yes, I guessed that's what it meant.
MOIRA: It's only too late that most people find that they can't give it all away like that, can't abdicate from the responsibility of forming a moral attitude.
LARRY: Mm.
FORESKIN: Feel like another — (drink)?
MOIRA: Overseas, people are more . . . mature. They'd thought about things, they'd made a few decisions, they'd asked 'why'?.
FORESKIN: Why not?
MOIRA: What do you mean?
FORESKIN: Well, that's the only question that's relevant here, isn't it? Whatever is not expressly prohibited is expressly permitted. You of all people should know that. Another gin and tonic?
MOIRA: Well, I . . .
FORESKIN: Fills in the seconds. The void.
MOIRA: Smart bastard.
FORESKIN: How's yours Larry?

LARRY: I'm right thanks Seymour.

FORESKIN *exits with his own and* MOIRA'S *glass.*

LARRY: You've travelled a bit then.
MOIRA: Yes. Enjoyed it, specially after I got home. Have you?
LARRY: No, always been a closet kiwi, or something-a-ruther. I never wanted to be, but what other kind is there in this country? Seems you have to leave it to be able to love it.
MOIRA: Don't worry, there's only two ways to enjoy travel. By proxy or in retrospect. Just listen to me and you'll get all the bullshit and none of the pain. Anyway, it's not the great OE they're all rushing to like lemmings. It's the great OP they're all rushing from.
LARRY: Don't know what either of them stand for, I'm afraid.
MOIRA: Overseas Experience and Oedipal Pressure.
LARRY: Oh. I seem to be able to bring that out in people.
MOIRA: What's that?
LARRY: My own ignorance.
MOIRA: Ha!

MOIRA *touches* LARRY'S *arm.*

Relax, you're speaking to an arrogant overbearing lady who doesn't know when to shut up.
LARRY: You're very . . . liberated.
MOIRA: Try to be.

Pause

Aren't you?

LARRY: I don't feel liberated. I feel very . . . sort of constrained. I feel there might have been more chance for me . . . nowadays.

Pause

The good old times. They never were, you know. It's just the merciful tendency of the mind to forget the worst of the pain. That's probably why I remember rugby so fondly.

Pause

MOIRA: Listen misery-guts, how about a dance? Let's make a bright romantic spot in the midst of all this turgid ockerism.
LARRY: There's no music.
MOIRA: Won't need any. We'll do the prison shuffle, I know it well. Hold me.

MOIRA steps closer to LARRY. LARRY is hesitant, but takes MOIRA rather stiffly in his arms.

LARRY: What about Fore — Seymour? I really don't want to step on anyone's toes.
MOIRA: As long as they're not mine Larry.

They begin dancing slowly around the verandah.

For all his poetry in motion, Seymour doesn't dance. One of his failings. When the rest of us were in the bible class dance with sweaty armpits and acne, the ineffable Seymour was sitting outside revving his V8, the wolf waiting for the bored lambs to wander from the fold.

LARRY: Really? Seymour?
MOIRA: Mm. And as a lamb I was more bored than most.
LARRY: Willingly to the slaughter, eh?
MOIRA: Just a little death, as they say. And a long time ago.
LARRY: You can be a rather shocking young lady.
MOIRA: Particularly for a Moira. You know, I never did like that name. It always conjured up visions of acne, glasses, and virginity in perpetuity.
LARRY: Yes, it does.

He laughs.

MOIRA: I thought of changing it, then I thought 'Why? Am I not strong enough to create my own image, to be master of my own fate?' . . . I'm sorry Larry, do I frighten you? I frighten a lot of men, I can tell you. Except Seymour. Frightened men and antagonised ladies I leave in my wake.
LARRY: But not Seymour?
MOIRA: Wish I could absolutely terrify him. But no.

Pause. MOIRA *stops dancing.* LARRY *disengages.*

LARRY: Brave of us telling all this. I don't usually drink so much.
MOIRA: Nor me. I can be quite mousey, sober. Drunk, I'm brilliant. Feel brilliant.
LARRY: Why don't we have the courage of our convictions? Or even convictions, that'd be a start. My deep dark secret seems to be common knowledge anyway. Even closets have ears.

In the background, the boat-races have ceased, and rude rugby songs begin. The songs continue as an audial background. CLEAN *lurches on to the stage, followed by* IRISH *and* MEAN, *who are trying to restrain him, dissuade him.* CLEAN *grabs* LARRY *by the shoulders, turning to see that his audience is attentive.*

CLEAN: Larry. Larry. Listen, how do you blow out a candle Larry?

LARRY *tries again to disengage from* CLEAN.

Poof!

CLEAN *almost spits in* LARRY'S *face, then lets go, belches terribly, and staggers toward the rail of the verandah. He hangs over the rail for some seconds, eyes rolling, his body obviously in some indecision about whether or not to vomit.* IRISH *and* MEAN *return to the party.*

MOIRA: Heartburn?
CLEAN: Eh? What the . . . oh, fluff. Whose fluff are you?
MOIRA: No one's.

ACT 2

> *Pause, while this registers.* CLEAN *labours into a standing position, turns away from the rail and begins advancing towards* MOIRA. LARRY *is still watching, with concern.*

CLEAN: No one's eh? So what's a nice girl like you doing out here? Or maybe you're not such a nice girl, eh?

> LARRY *moves towards* MOIRA *protectively.*

MOIRA: Hold it! I'm not a stray, all right?
CLEAN: That's what I asked you. You said — (you weren't with)
MOIRA: I'm with Seymour — Foreskin, sorry.
CLEAN: Oh, the edjimicated fluff. I'm into fluff in a big way.
MOIRA: You mean you'd like to be.

> CLEAN *moves again towards* MOIRA.

Don't come any closer. I've got a scream like a siren.

CLEAN: Okay, okay, settle down.

> LARRY *begins to realise that perhaps he's not needed and begins easing himself out.*

LARRY: Well, I'd better go back and check on everything.

> *There's a crash inside as a plate or glass breaks.*

I can't help feeling like an insurance assessor when I go back in there. You'll be all right then, Moira, you don't want to come — (and have a bite)

MOIRA: Fine Larry. I'll wait for Seymour, and my drink. Thanks.
LARRY: Well —
CLEAN: See you later Larry.

> LARRY *exits.*

CLEAN: Well now, what's a lovely piece of fluff like you doing with a wanker like Foreskin, anyway? Going to waste I bet.
MOIRA: He's interesting, quite apart from anything else. I like him, don't you?
CLEAN: He's a fucken twerp. Cost us the game today.
MOIRA: Oh. All for one and one for all. I thought rugby was camaraderie, team spirit, all that collective hogwash. I think Seymour told me that.
CLEAN: Let's talk about you. What do you do with yourself?
MOIRA: When?
CLEAN: Eh?
MOIRA: Rather a personal question.
CLEAN: Oh, I getcha. Spunky chick, eh? I mean what do you do for a crust?
MOIRA: Are you sure you haven't seen me before . . . cuntstable?
CLEAN: How do you know that? Oh, Foreskin.
MOIRA: No, we've more interesting things to talk about, I can assure you. Tell me, don't you find it awfully boring, standing there by the door all day, opening and shutting it for poor bastards who've stolen a cold pie, propping up old drunks in the dock so they can hear the Magistrate say, 'This man needs a doctor'? I mean, I've often wondered, before tonight, what it is you people think about all day. The newspapers are screaming that you're under siege, that you're thin on the ground — I would have said thick — and yet you're arresting people for using words which most policemen routinely use to describe their wives, and you're arresting people for pissing in public places — christ, Europe, the cradle of civilisation, is awash with people pissing with gay abandon. I mean it must really be a job with enormous satisfaction . . . I've acted for some of the 16- and 17-year-olds your heavies have worked over.
CLEAN: A lawyer, you're a fucken lawyer! I've seen you, glasses —
MOIRA: Manual need, not visual — when stumped, fiddle with glasses.
CLEAN: Christ — well, I wasn't to know.
MOIRA: What?
CLEAN: What?

ACT 2

MOIRA: What weren't you to know?
CLEAN: That you're . . . who you are.
MOIRA: That I'm a person, rather than a bit of fluff? Or a lawyer, rather than a mere person?
CLEAN: Listen, I don't want to get into any of that shit.
MOIRA: Shit? I thought we were talking about women. You did say you were into women. Or was it shit?

Pause

CLEAN: I'll be seeing you.
MOIRA: You haven't answered my question.
CLEAN: Don't threaten me!

Pause

Look . . . I know what you're on about — 'What passes through the brain of our Mr Plod on duty?' 'I wonder what a spider thinks about sitting in his web on a slow day?' I don't think about 'why am I here' and I'm not apologising for it.

MOIRA: Wouldn't dream of asking you to.
CLEAN: I'm grateful to be there, I can tell you. I was a mug.
MOIRA: What kind of mug?
CLEAN: You see a lot of them. The converted, born again lot — hare fucken krishnas, children of God, or Moon, whatever.
MOIRA: You? Really? I can't picture you in saffron. What were you?
CLEAN: A born again golden product.
MOIRA: Oh?
CLEAN: Pyramid selling. Positivism. Now there's a big word for our Mr Plod. How to make the world seem rosy. They're all pushing the same shit.
MOIRA: What happened?
CLEAN: Two and a half years ago I was twenty-six, had a wife and kid to support, and a house full of soap-suds to show for it. Bankrupt.
MOIRA: So you joined the force.

CLEAN: Seemed natural, for an ex-army grunt. It's got its good points, that kind of life. You obey orders, get your dough at the end of the week. You're looked after, no worries.

MOIRA: I can see you're a real idealist.

CLEAN: No, but then I've done the rounds, lady. It takes a while to see how the world runs. I'm a slow learner, but I don't make the same mistake twice. I've even got my own philosophy — there, that's another word with more than two syllables, doing well, aren't we? I was in Viet Nam. Came back with a bit of dough put aside, wanted to work for myself, make a business. So I made the wrong move — poof! — nothing — well, a house full of soap-suds. But I did learn a bit from Nam. I just made the mistake of thinking civvy street was different. Y'know, those yanks are the boys. They've got it by the balls. You stick it to them, that's their philosophy. Right up the arse. You stick it to them till they've got turds coming out their nostrils.

Pause. MOIRA *shivers.*

MOIRA: Who's 'them'?

CLEAN: Whoever. Whatever. Everything's there for the taking, not the asking.

MOIRA: Oh.

CLEAN: I won't be with the force forever, either. Not after I make a name for myself in rugby.

MOIRA: I thought rugby was amateur. You wouldn't get much change out of that surely?

CLEAN: Oh, it's amateur all right. But you'd be surprised. It's not the rugby that's commercial, it's the name. Once you've made the name, you can travel on it. Just think how many name players are flogging the roads between here and Kaitaia for everything from shit paper to ladies' underwear.

MOIRA: You do have some curious associations. You'd like that?

CLEAN: It's easy. More future than propping up drunks in the dock, and it's easier on the varicose veins. I'm no fool, despite appearances, and how I carry on for the benefit of those idiots in there. I'm twenty-nine. I use a roll of electrical tape instead of ligaments for one knee, this shoulder has been tied once and dropped twice since, and both ankles are so stuffed they don't even swell up any more. It's late. Not much time left, maybe two seasons at the outside, if I'm going to make it.

Pause

Shocked lady?
MOIRA: You could say that.
CLEAN: Lawyers shouldn't ask questions they don't know the answers to. Isn't that the rule? The distance between me and you is a fucken world, if you'll excuse the language.

Enter FORESKIN *upstage with drinks, unseen by either* MOIRA *or* CLEAN, *but moving into* CLEAN's *line of vision.*

MOIRA: It's not the fucks that I take exception to.
CLEAN: Yeah, maybe I know that. You're some lady.
MOIRA: Woman.
CLEAN: Yeah, woman.

CLEAN *sees* FORESKIN.

Bits of fluff are a lot easier to handle.

MOIRA: Be careful of high winds.

CLEAN *looks slightly uncomfortable under* FORESKIN's *stare, and retreats as* FORESKIN *advances.*

CLEAN: Well, better get back to the boys. See you.

CLEAN *exits under* FORESKIN's *stare.*

FORESKIN: What was all that about?
MOIRA: I've just had the misfortune of meeting Clean — is it? — On what some people might call a one-to-one basis, although I think that's an exaggerated ratio.

FORESKIN: Oh.

MOIRA: I've seen pigs at a trough with more style than that.

FORESKIN: Take it easy Moira, or at least keep your voice down.

MOIRA: Oh, don't worry about that, they only understand grunts and belches.

FORESKIN: Moira what the hell do you want from these people?

MOIRA: Normality, warmth, empathy, a little communication of interests, ideas — no more than I'd expect from any gathering of reasonably aware human beings.

FORESKIN: Moira, you've got to forget all that Aquarian hype. What people like you don't seem to realise is that the effect of the Sixties on the great miasma amounted to an extra inch of whisker on the end of a Taranaki farmer's side-board.

MOIRA: People like me? Care to define that?

FORESKIN: Let's just leave it.

MOIRA: I want to know what you really meant by 'people like me'.

FORESKIN: All right. I meant effete intellectuals like you, like us, trendy lefties or trendy fascists, makes no difference, who indulge in profound discussions with esoteric peers, pick over the issues like a pack of erudite hens tossing stale wheat back and forth, too satiated to know what it really tastes like. We indulge in polite proselytising bounded by petty rules of good form — nothing more than gentility masquerading as reason. Gut feelings, bed-rock passions — honesty — have nothing to do with it. We're playing parlour games, Moira, which have nothing to do with reality. Our reality is here, not in the bouquet of a '72 Cabernet, or in meaningless landscapes of the Shotover, or in eternal variations of god-boy-as-simple-kiwi — nor in the people who create them. This is the heart and the bowels of this country, too strong and foul and vital for reduction to bouquets, or oils, or words. If you think they're pigs, then you'd better look closer, and get used to the smell, because their smell is your smell, it's they who decide for us which road, what speed, how far, and who drives — they decide how and why we live, and tolerate us for the rest, or best.

MOIRA: Stop it! I don't believe it, I can't believe that you do.

FORESKIN: I've always believed it. But it used to be quite comforting. Perhaps that's what I'm mourning.

Pause. MOIRA *goes to* FORESKIN. *They embrace.*

MOIRA: Sometimes I have this feeling that I don't know you at all.

Pause

Why the funny names . . . Foreskin? I never noticed it.
FORESKIN: Are they that unusual . . . Honey?
MOIRA: All right.
FORESKIN: Progress has a lot of chops to answer for — trees, animals, sensibilities of all kinds, what's a piece of skin?
MOIRA: Can cover a lot of sensibilities.
FORESKIN: Ha ha.
MOIRA: Well?
FORESKIN: Lost. Pretersensual pain — the chop I missed and have always been bound for. Perhaps I'm crediting them with too much.
MOIRA: I can't decide which are worse — your childish jokes when you're not serious, or your riddles when you are. And Clean?
FORESKIN: Clean? As in squeaky clean, or Mr Clean the soap-suds man. Or P.C. Clean, keeping the dirt off our streets. Or Clean 'n Jerk, take your pick, Clean or the jerk, get it?

MOIRA *disengages and steps back.*

MOIRA: Oh, we're back to that. Hiding again.
FORESKIN: Or clean, as in wound or kill — clean kill, takes no prisoners, not even superiors.
MOIRA: Now the riddles.
FORESKIN: He's a riddle. An ugly one.
MOIRA: He'll do well in the force, he's got the same look as all those C.I.B. Dees — hard, cold, dead, as if what those eyes have looked at, or for, in people, has killed the light in them. None of

the criminals I've seen scare me half as much. He makes me feel I've had a very sheltered life.

FORESKIN: You have.

MOIRA: What do you mean?

FORESKIN: Rich daddy. If you haven't had to wonder where your next buck is coming from, then you've missed out on the major preoccupation of the waking hours of the western world.

MOIRA: Well, would you have refused?

FORESKIN: Nope.

Enter LARRY *to a burst of sound from upstage — general enthusiasm over supper.*

LARRY: Ah there you are, you two. Supper's on, you'll find it right under the scrum.

FORESKIN: Care for a pinch of pav deah?

MOIRA: No thanks.

FORESKIN: Perhaps a small tumescent cheerio?

MOIRA: Get away!

MOIRA *goes on ahead.* LARRY *approaches* FORESKIN.

LARRY: I like her. . . . Any more news of Ken?

FORESKIN: No, we'll give the hospital another ring.

Exit MOIRA, LARRY *and* FORESKIN. *Pause. Enter* TUPPER, *with a can of beer and a plate overflowing with everything from pavlova to legs of chicken.* TUPPER *is looking a little devious and pleased with himself, and is obviously intent on finding a quiet place to gorge himself without fear of distraction or censure.* TUPPER *arranges the can and the plate carefully on the table, undoes his belt and the top button of his trousers, pats his stomach in anticipation, then piles straight into a large slice of pavlova. Enter* CLEAN, *belching, with a can of beer and a plate similar to* TUPPER'S.

CLEAN: G'day Tee. Nothing like a bit of a feed to settle the guts down.

ACT 2

> TUPPER *is at first unable to reply. The following conversation stutters along between mouthfulls.*

TUPPER: Man after me own heart. By the way, Clean, good speech, good speech son. Mentioned all the right things, did very well, wouldn't have guessed it was your first skipper's speech.

CLEAN: Simple enough Tupper, no worries.

TUPPER: Yeah. There's one thing though, Clean. Very small thing but I may as well mention it, as it's a matter of principle with me, you know, team policy, that sort of thing.

CLEAN: Sure Tee, go ahead.

TUPPER: Well, it's just that, win or lose, victory or capostrophe, I really don't think individuals should be mentioned.

CLEAN: Don't remember mentioning anyone by name, other than the referee.

TUPPER: You did mention Foreskin — just the once, mind you. About him not passing the ball that time.

CLEAN: Cost us the bloody game that. Jesus, I hardly said a thing, he deserves a far worse fate than that, and I'd give it to him if — (I had half a)

TUPPER: Now now, Clean, easy son. Nothing can be laid completely at the feet of any one player. If someone else had scored a try we wouldn't have needed that one, would we?

CLEAN: You've been talking too long to Irish.

> CLEAN *stands and surveys the verandah. He goes upstage and, with his back to the audience, makes to urinate off the verandah on to the garden.* TUPPER *has to crane around in his chair to talk to* CLEAN.

TUPPER: I'm not trying to excuse Foreskin at all. But, publicly as it were, none of us should be seen pulling the other one down. You're an army man yourself Clean, you know what I'm talking about, camder — ah, you know, the old camerder — ah, comradeship, the common cause.

Pause

CLEAN: Sure Tupper, sure. The old army, eh? Well, that's okay publicly, but privately, between me and you, what are we going to do about that cunt?
TUPPER: What do you mean?

CLEAN returns to his chair and his food.

CLEAN: Well, it's no good letting him fuck up the team — and you've got to admit, he's really an unsettling influence. You said so yourself at training the other night. Look what he did to your team-talk.
TUPPER: Oh, we sorted that out all right.
CLEAN: The fuck you did. You and Foreskin might have sorted it out, but what about the guys who heard it all, then went home thinking about it? What impression did they have of Foreskin's respect for you, the coach? What impression did they carry away with them of your famous camaraderie? It's showing on the field, Tupper. We should have been good for 20 points in against those Ngapuk bumpkins. Instead of that, Foreskin takes away all our psyche before the game, then manages to lose the game for us on the field too. I don't know what your army was like Tupper, but in mine we couldn't afford selfish pencil-neck free spirits. That guy's a fucken menace to any team.
TUPPER: Oh he's a good boy really. Good material deep down there. Just been led astray by some of these univarsity roosters, I'd say.
CLEAN: Well it's your head will be on the chopping block now Ken's gone.
TUPPER: Oh Ken'll be back.
CLEAN: Gone, Tupper. He won't be worth a plugged nickel for the rest of this season at least. I can't be expected to take any responsibility for results as captain while Foreskin's in the team, Tupper I'm telling you that straight.
TUPPER: Look, I'll have a talk to the lad, Clean. Set him straight. We can't just abandon him like that. Might be his last chance to be one of the boys.

Pause

ACT 2

Maybe I could work on him through that sheila of his. She seems a nice homely sort of type. Not like those other floozies he gets around with — yeah, I'll have a yarn to her.

CLEAN *gets to his feet with his plate, ready to leave.*

CLEAN: I think you'll find her pretty easy to influence.
TUPPER: You think so?
CLEAN: Putty in your hands, Tupper.
TUPPER: Won't hurt to use a bit of the old sly, a bit of the old cunning, will it? What's her name again?
CLEAN: Ah, Myrtle, Tupper. Myrtle, I'm pretty sure that was it.

CLEAN *exits, calling out to* MOIRA *that there's someone on the verandah who wants to talk to her.* TUPPER *loses himself in his food again, and doesn't notice* MOIRA'S *entrance until he's finished off the plate. When he does see her, he's embarrassed, half rises to his feet, knocks his plate over, tries to do up his trouser button and belt.*

TUPPER: Ah . . . g'day . . . ah, evening.
MOIRA: It is, isn't it?
TUPPER: What — ah — pardon?
MOIRA: A good evening.
TUPPER: Oh, yeah-s, certainly is. Lovely evening. Be ideal . . . for a spot of . . . floundering. Romantic.
MOIRA: I never thought of floundering in that light before.
TUPPER: Well, you don't want too much. That moon's about right, I'd say.
MOIRA: I mean I'd never thought of floundering as being particularly romantic.
TUPPER: Floundering? Romantic? Pig's arse. About as much romance in floundering as two Irish sailors on shore leave on St — sorry Myrtle, do apologise. Tend to get carried away.
MOIRA: That's quite all right, Tipper.
TUPPER: Tupper, Myrtle, Tupper. Tipper sounds like a dago waiter bending and scraping like a catholic warming up for confession. Ha ha. Call me Tee for short.

MOIRA: Thank you, and you can call me Moira, even for short.
TUPPER: Moira? But Clean said — (your name was)
MOIRA: Have you just been talking to that — to Clean?
TUPPER: Oh, just in passing, you know. About the . . . team, the weather, that sort of thing.
MOIRA: I suppose he'd just about pass muster on those subjects, and floundering.
TUPPER: Doesn't strike me as the fishing type, somehow.
MOIRA: No, I'm sure he'd have more serious mayhem in mind.
TUPPER: Can't imagine anything more peaceful than fishing.
MOIRA: Kills fish.
TUPPER: Thought you did a bit of floundering yourself.
MOIRA: Whatever gave you that idea — do I look so inadequate?
TUPPER: No, you said something about it being the right kind of moon for it. Sounded to me like you'd had a bit of experience.
MOIRA: Perhaps we'd be better off just looking at the moon, rather than talking about it.
TUPPER: Waste of bloody time doing either, I'd say.
MOIRA: Well, what would you like to talk about? I'm not much good on rugby, I'm afraid.
TUPPER: Oh no, not rugby . . . necessarily. A bit of a yarn, few personalities man-to- . . . well, this and that, you know.
MOIRA: The aberrant Foreskin?
TUPPER: Seymour? Oh, he's not that bad.
MOIRA: Aberrant, nevertheless.
TUPPER: Not many of them play rugby. Besides, I couldn't care less if he was a Maori as long as he pulls his weight. Na, na, listen. We can't be too hard on the boy, calling him names like that. I've known him for a long time, and I know that deep down he's a good boy. He's like a healthy engine, just raring to go, but right now there's a load of shit on the plugs. See what I mean?
MOIRA: Shit on the plugs, you'd say.
TUPPER: Or too much of a gap between the points — contact gap, know what I mean, eh? Being the kind of lad he is.
MOIRA: What kind of 'lad' do you think he is Tupper, apart from having fouled plugs and points?
TUPPER: I think he's basically a good boy, salt of the earth.

MOIRA: More pepper than salt, perhaps.
TUPPER: Na, na, he'd be all right — all he needs is a good woman behind him, to settle him down, give him the odd prod in the right direction.
MOIRA: Which direction?
TUPPER: The footy field — training on Tuesdays and Thursdays. I'll take care of the lad.
MOIRA: So that's basically all that's wrong with him, deep down? Misses the odd training run?
TUPPER: Na. Doesn't pàss when he's s'posed to. Talks too fucken much. Bad influence, even if most of the others can't understand what he's saying half the time.
MOIRA: What do you want me to do? Where do I fit into your grand scheme?
TUPPER: Talk to him. Be more ... helpful. I don't want to get personal, but it wouldn't do any harm letting him give wee Arnold a trot occasionally.

Pause

MOIRA: Wee Arnold?
TUPPER: Yeah, you know ... it'd stop him chasing round town for it. You'd get your cake, too.
MOIRA: My cake?
TUPPER: Yeah, once he's settled down, getting his oats regular like, well, chucking a rock's the next thing he'll think of.
MOIRA: Chucking a block?
TUPPER: Rock. Ring on the finger. Rock.
MOIRA: You think that's what I want from him?
TUPPER: What else would you want from him? Stands to reason.
MOIRA: I've never heard so many anachronistic pigs in all my life.
TUPPER: Steady on there, Myrtle. Calling a man a pig's a bit rough, whatever breed it is. What did I say?
MOIRA: You really don't know, do you? You people! This rugby scene is like a junkyard for obsolete mentalities, this is where you're all hiding, waiting for the real world to go away.
TUPPER: Now hold on, some of us fought in the war —

MOIRA: And you still are! Do you realise how long ago that really was? What's happened since?

TUPPER: Sweet fuck all that's good as far as I can see.

MOIRA: What about — what about the breaking down of stereotypes, so that people can really be themselves.

TUPPER: Just confuses people. Man wants to know where he stands.

MOIRA: Sensitivity, awareness, look at how things have changed outside —

TUPPER: Balls! Lot of lily-arsed bastards who don't know whether to stand or squat when they go to the grot. Tuesdays and Thursdays down at the clubhouse'd do wonders for them. Potential's still there. It's not too late. That's all I'm trying to tell you about Foreskin.

MOIRA: I agree with you on one thing. The potential is still there, god knows how. And you can be assured Tupper, I'll make every possible sacrifice, lay down my body for Queen and country more often than is absolutely necessary, give wee Arnold a veritable gallop, to ensure that Seymour moves in the right direction.

TUPPER: Well! Couldn't ask for more than that. Certainly helps to have a bit of a talk. Don't you worry, we won't abandon the lad, he'll come right yet. Nice talking to you Myrtle, any problems, just give me a yell, I've been around, I know the score.

MOIRA: Thank you, Tipper, but I hope to be out of earshot.

TUPPER: Tupper, Myrtle, Tupper.

MOIRA: Good luck with the floundering.

TUPPER: Eh? Oh, yeah.

Enter FORESKIN, *as* TUPPER *is scurrying out.*

FORESKIN: Oh Tee, I want to have a word with you.

TUPPER *stops, harried.*

TUPPER: Aaah . . . later son, later. Got to take a piss — my bladder's the size of a football.

TUPPER *exits.* FORESKIN *looks after him, puzzled.*

FORESKIN: Well.

Pause

MOIRA: Well. How's . . . ah . . . wee Arnold these days?
FORESKIN: What?
MOIRA: I mean, would you say that he's, um, getting enough exercise?
FORESKIN: Is that what he's been on about? No wonder he was looking so bloody guilty.

MOIRA sidles closer, and puts her hand on FORESKIN'S crutch. She bends over, so she is addressing his crutch.

MOIRA: Well now, wee Arnold (let's see what we can do for the common cause).

MEAN and his wife PAT enter as MOIRA is thus engrossed. MEAN and PAT have their coats on and are obviously ready to leave. MEAN is carrying a carry-cot.

PAT: Oh. Lose something dear?

FORESKIN and MOIRA disengage hurriedly.

FORESKIN: Moira, meet Mean, is actually clean — small attempt at team irony there.
MEAN: Hullo, Seymour, pleased to meet you, Moira. Don't think you've met the wife before, have you, Seymour? Seymour, Pat, Pat, Seymour. He's our fullback Pat.
PAT: Oh yes, I have seen you playing the odd time, now that I remember. You're easy to see back there. It's no good trying to watch Fred, I can never tell which arms and legs are his amongst all those fronts.
MEAN: Forwards, dear.
PAT: Oh . . . yes.
FORESKIN: This is Moira, Pat. She's not much of a fan either.

PAT: Oh, aren't you, dear?

MOIRA: I saw a bumper sticker in the States that sums up my attitude to the game — 'In rugby there are no winners, only survivors.'

PAT: I quite agree, Moira, you wouldn't credit how many days' work Fred has lost through silly rugby injuries.

MEAN: Ah, get away with you woman.

PAT: And what about young Ken lying in hospital? I'd like to see you convince him that it's not a dangerous game.

FORESKIN: Oh, they already did.

PAT: What?

FORESKIN: Convince him. In fact they guaranteed him.

MEAN: I didn't see how it happened. Well, I saw Ken get caught in possession, he covered up, we were all there in support for the maul, and that's the last I see till the whistle for the lineout. Then I look around and there he is, lying there. So still. Usually there's some movement, a few moans, but not a thing. I suppose he must have gone down and collected a boot. Bad luck twice in a row like that. Did you see anything from back there Seymour?

FORESKIN: I did actually. You're the first who's wanted to know. It was a kick in the head, a deliberate, blatant, Clean kick.

MEAN: Did you see which one of them did it?

FORESKIN: It was Clean all right.

MEAN: Yes, but who did it? Those Ngapuk lads seem such a decent bunch basically. There wasn't a spot of trouble in the whole game, then suddenly, kapow — this! It just doesn't make sense. Couldn't have been deliberate Seymour. You can usually feel those things building up.

FORESKIN: This has been building up for a long time Fred, if only you knew.

MEAN: Well, I've been playing Ngapuk for eleven years now. Always seemed a decent bunch of lads to me.

FORESKIN: I'm not doubting them, Fred.

PAT: I hope Ken will be all right. Cathy will be worried sick. And what happens to the business while he's in hospital?

MEAN: Oh, he'll probably be out later tonight. They just put him in there for observation.

ACT 2   79

FORESKIN: He's still in a coma. Never came round. I rang the hospital ten minutes ago.
PAT: Stupid game!
FORESKIN: Just stupid people.
MEAN: A couple of weeks more, then you'll have your peace, woman.
FORESKIN: Retiring?
MEAN: It's getting a bit much. I'm not enjoying it as I used to. Saturdays won't seem the same, though. I may coach the youngsters in a year or two. Oh, Pat here will miss the social side of things too, without a doubt.
PAT: It's sometimes a bit difficult finding a baby-sitter, you know. And I don't think this is the sort of place to bring children.
FORESKIN: Just give me a yell Pat, I'd be happy to do it.
PAT: I wouldn't dream of asking you Seymour. That way, you couldn't be here either. Don't be silly.
FORESKIN: Might be sillier to come.
PAT: To tell you the truth, we're not too fussy about these either. Wee Andrew here makes a good excuse for leaving early.
MEAN: That's quite enough of the trade secrets for tonight, dear. Well, we'd better be on our way, long drive.
PAT: Nice meeting you Seymour, Moira.
MOIRA: Bye Pat. Fred.
MEAN: Goodbye Moira. See you on Tuesday night, Seymour.
FORESKIN: Goodbye Fred.

FRED pauses slightly at FORESKIN'S response. MEAN and PAT exit.

MOIRA: Nice people

FORESKIN is gazing out from the verandah, his mind elsewhere.

FORESKIN: Mm.

Pause

MOIRA: Can we go? — they're getting out.
FORESKIN: We can't go home yet.

MOIRA: Why not?
FORESKIN: I've got to . . . sort it out.
MOIRA: Let's just run — get away from this whole thing. Run while you still can!
FORESKIN: Where to? You? The female panacea?
MOIRA: That's not fair.
FORESKIN: I know. Moira, please not now.
MOIRA: Not now, not yesterday, not tomorrow. Not ever! You're hiding again. Selfish bastard!

FORESKIN *turns to face* MOIRA.

FORESKIN: What are we talking about Moira?
MOIRA: Can't you compromise, just once? Think of me?
FORESKIN: You?
MOIRA: Me. As opposed to the imbecilic Tupper, or the moronic Clean. Is that asking too much?
FORESKIN: It's not a competition Moira. You're not enough. They're not enough. But that's not even the point. This is my earth. I'm rooted in it, whatever my fine aspirations.

Pause

Look, I can understand if you don't want to stay. You don't have to stay.

MOIRA: I want to go.
FORESKIN: It's your car.
MOIRA: Jesus christ!

Pause. FORESKIN *turns away to look out from the verandah. After a little while,* MOIRA *sees that* FORESKIN *is not looking or responding.*

Fuck you!

MOIRA *exits, leaving* FORESKIN *alone on stage for a moment.* CLEAN *and* IRISH *enter, drunkenly.*

ACT 2   81

CLEAN: Foreskin! Where've you been hiding all night, you piking cunt? Been out chundering, can't hold your piss, eh?
FORESKIN: Is that what it takes?
CLEAN: Eh?
FORESKIN: What does it take, Clean?

> FORESKIN *approaches* CLEAN. IRISH *attempts to mediate.*

IRISH: Now listen boys, let's not get too — (intellectual)
FORESKIN: We'll see what it takes. A little test.

> FORESKIN *grabs* IRISH *and puts on a huckster voice. The following scene is to be played vaudeville style, particularly after Irish clicks to the 'Brucie' character.* IRISH *is fairly drunk and giggling throughout the walnut game.*

> Now Irish, pretend you're a good keen kiwi lad instead of a wasted Irish git.

IRISH: Bit of a come-down, but okay.

> LARRY *enters.*

CLEAN: Watch it Irish, it'll be Zen or fucken Shakespeare.
FORESKIN: Na Clean, you might even be able to handle the last bit.

> *To* IRISH:

> Now, Brucie . . .

IRISH: Ah!

> *He slumps down to his impression of a gormless yobbo.*

FORESKIN: Now Brucie, what do you want to be more than anything in the world?
IRISH: Straight?

> FORESKIN *clips his ear.*

FORESKIN: Too intellectual Brucie, try again.

> IRISH *gets into the act, begins drooping again, shuffles his feet, puts on the newzealandese, beams idiotically.*

IRISH: Well, ah, I wanna be, ah, one of the boys.
FORESKIN: Right Brucie. And what do the boys do, Brucie?
IRISH: Play footie.
FORESKIN: Right Brucie. Now Brucie, what position eh?

> IRISH *reverts to* IRISH.

IRISH: Missionary, I'm more Roman than catholic.

> FORESKIN *twists* IRISH *by the ear and makes him turn towards* LARRY.

FORESKIN: Now now Brucie, don't get smart.

> *To* LARRY: You sir, you this boy's father?

> LARRY *enters into the game, effectively isolating* CLEAN, *who stands brooding.*

LARRY: Yes sir.
FORESKIN: Does it read or write?
LARRY: Well sir, no. Draws a pretty diagram, adds up the odd figure, builds a great little house with its blocks and plasticine, but no, does not read or write.
FORESKIN: Tsk tsk, not a back then, is it? No chance for fullback. I'm afraid, Brucie, the higher arts of the game are beyond you.

> IRISH *acts disappointed and goes to wander away.* FORESKIN *gets a walnut from a plate on the table and grabs him again.*

FORESKIN: Now now Brucie, we'll find you a place, don't you worry. Now Brucie, see this walnut?

FORESKIN *waves the walnut in front of* IRISH, *then carefully puts the walnut on his head. Then he holds both hands, palms open, towards* IRISH.

    Now Brucie, for flanker or No. 8, concentrate. Ready?
IRISH: Yep.
FORESKIN: Right, which hand is the walnut in?

IRISH *struggles mightily. He grabs* FORESKIN'S *right hand and examines it.*

IRISH: Na. Not here. Not in this one.

IRISH *drops* FORESKIN'S *right hand and turns to* FORESKIN'S *left hand. He pulls* FORESKIN'S *hand towards him. As he does so,* FORESKIN *swivels slightly.*

IRISH: Na. Not in this one either.

IRISH *scratches his head, then looks behind* FORESKIN. *Suddenly grunts in elation, and feels with his hands along* FORESKIN'S *back until he reaches* FORESKIN'S *right hand again. Examines it minutely.*

IRISH: Piss on it. Not in this fucker neither. Jesus. You couldn't sort of hold them all out in front together could you, so's I can get a good gander at them all at once?

FORESKIN *takes the walnut from his head.*

FORESKIN: Sorry son. Got to move on to the donkeys I'm afraid. Concentrate Brucie, for second row, for lock, where's the walnut?

FORESKIN *closes one palm, the one holding the walnut. The other he leaves open and obviously empty. He holds both hands towards* IRISH, *waving the closed one obviously.* IRISH *grins in relief.*

IRISH: Ah, you can't fool me this time.

> IRISH *ignores* FORESKIN'S *hands and grabs for* FORESKIN'S *hair.* FORESKIN *ducks his head so Irish can look.*

IRISH: Jesus, can't see it for the life of me.
FORESKIN: Oh dear, oh dear. Well, that only leaves the front row Brucie, prop or hooker, if you pass this one. No brain no pain, but we had to be sure. Now concentrate Brucie, if you miss this one the only place left is the Rugby Union.
IRISH: Oh no, not the Rugby Union!

> IRISH *walks away in mock utter dejection.* FORESKIN *grabs him again.* FORESKIN *holds both hands up, palms open. The walnut is clearly visible, held against one palm by the thumb, and, again,* FORESKIN *waves it obviously under* IRISH'S *nose.*

FORESKIN: Now Brucie, where's the walnut?

> IRISH *stares intently at the palms, one by one.*

IRISH: A walnut, you reckon?

> CLEAN *intervenes violently, pulling* IRISH *by the shoulder.*

CLEAN: That's enough Irish, you fucken galoot! What the fuck are you trying to do Foreskin?
FORESKIN: Teach him to recognise nuts.
LARRY: Good on you Foreskin.

> CLEAN *turns on* LARRY.

CLEAN: Shut up you fucken queer!
LARRY: I don't think you're in any position to call anyone names with Kenny lying in hospital.
CLEAN: I'll bust your fucken head in — (you jumped up)

CLEAN *graps* LARRY *by the collar, ready to punch him.* FORESKIN *moves to intervene.*

FORESKIN: Like you did Kenny's?

Pause

IRISH *steps in between* FORESKIN *and* CLEAN.

IRISH: No, come on lads, we don't want —

FORESKIN *pushes* IRISH *out of the way, which leaves* CLEAN *and* FORESKIN *confronting each other, on the brink of a fight.*

FORESKIN: No! No! The masks have been on long enough. Let's drop them, stop this masquerade in the name of team spirit. I'm sick and tired of it!
CLEAN: Give it away then. If you can't hack it, give it away!
FORESKIN: Clean, what the fuck is this game we're playing? Larry, get Tupper in here.

LARRY *moves to the door but* CLEAN *blocks him.*

CLEAN: Leave Tupper out of it!
FORESKIN: He's the coach Clean, he's got to be in on it.
CLEAN: He's just an old fart left over from the Second World War. He thinks that was all about chivalry and camaraderie too.
FORESKIN: He believes, Clean, in rugby, in his players, in you, for instance.
CLEAN: Then he's a fucken stupid old fart. The days of the rip-shit-or-bust coach are gone. He's a dying breed. There wouldn't be one cunt in this team who takes him seriously.
FORESKIN: I do.
CLEAN: Well, one cunt.

Pause. CLEAN *looks at* IRISH, LARRY *and* FORESKIN *in turn.*

CLEAN: I've had enough of this shit, the game's due to start. Come on Irish.

IRISH *doesn't move.*

IRISH: Be with you in just a mo Clean.

Pause

CLEAN: Suit yourself.

> CLEAN *exits. Silence.* LARRY *sits wearily, looking into his glass. Upstage, not on the verandah, but visible and identifiable, a television set is switched on. The sound of a rugby commentary can be heard, and the subdued response of those listening and watching.*

IRISH: Just . . . play the game Foreskin, it's easy enough.
FORESKIN: I don't seem to know the rules any more, Irish. No, that's not it. I still know the rules, but they just don't seem . . . worth it.
IRISH: Worth what? Costs nothing to play along.
FORESKIN: That's where you're wrong Irish. It costs us all. It's costing me too much.
IRISH: Ah, now, Foreskin.
FORESKIN: No, look at us all Irish. Playing along, humouring each other, bullshit in one sustaining bullshit in the other. Tupper play-acting for the team's benefit, all you guys playing along for his benefit. I was the only one who believed the whole charade was serious. When does the charade stop?
IRISH: Well, if it's only a charade, why — (worry about)
FORESKIN: Because the results are the same, whether it's a charade or not. The values get fucked.
IRISH: Now come on —
FORESKIN: The values get fucked!

Pause

You know what Tupper said to me on Thursday night Irish? 'This is the best thing, the best experience these guys will ever have.' Irish, he believes that. And these guys just think it's shit.

Pause

What the fuck's wrong with me, Irish? I used to think it was more dangerous to spend too much time with those academics up at the university. I spend hours being lectured on the inauthentic voice in modern literature by academics who live life vicariously, through books and abstractions. I looked down on them, I thought they were cowards, cowering from the nitty-gritty.

IRISH: And now you find the nitty-gritty's a charade.
FORESKIN: Yeah. What the fuck's everyone hiding from? I mean, Jesus, who among us has not lived in a glasshouse, eh? — or thrown the odd stone? Well, I'm prepared to admit it, the whole sordid story of festering perversion — oh Lord I have sinned mightily — flagellate, flagellate.

On these two words FORESKIN *makes as if to whip himself on the back.*

— not so much against you — I'm sure you had more fun — but against the great Calvin ethic that governs this country. Oh yes, I've . . .
masticated in the dead of night
been inebriated during daylight hours
muttered cucken funt in public places
dropped the odd browny in dire circumstances amongst public park pongas
had warts in funny places
fornicated for the mere pleasure of it
and — worst of all — never a touch of guilt,
not even to heighten the enjoyment . . .
LARRY *has risen in alarm.*

Sorry Larry.

IRISH: That's better, me old son. Now that you're well again, I'll be off to watch the game, see me money disappear.

IRISH *exits gratefully.*

FORESKIN: Sorry Larry.

Pause

Have you seen Tupper?
LARRY: Can't say that I have recently. Last I saw of him he was in the lounge — (near the grog table)
FORESKIN: Tupper! Tupper!
LARRY: He's a bit morose, Seymour — (I don't know if it's a good idea).
FORESKIN: Tupper! Tupper!

TUPPER *enters.* LARRY *looks disconsolate, exits.* TUPPER *is very drunk and deliberate, and sways a little as he stands.*

TUPPER: Son.
FORESKIN: Dad.
TUPPER: Listen son.
FORESKIN: Yes Dad.
TUPPER: All joking aside.
FORESKIN: Best place for it.
TUPPER: I find it difficult to talk to you.
FORESKIN: With you.
TUPPER: I can't talk with you.
FORESKIN: Then let's whistle, like dolphins. All kinds of possibilities. Sonar Shakespeare. A choice of Grass or McGonagall by the whistling Tupper. Or Dostoevski in dangerous decibels. Or Tchaikovsky by sheepdog whistle —
TUPPER: F'god's sake Foreskin — (give us a break)
FORESKIN: The barriers would be down, a merger of the arts through puckered lips and hot air.
TUPPER: I don't understand you.

FORESKIN: You want to reduce me to your understanding Tupper, place me in the scheme of things in order to manipulate me for the greater glory of the team, and your ego, or alter ego. What you don't understand frightens you. I'm glad you can't reduce my world to your own narrow terms.

TUPPER: You've lost me.

FORESKIN: I didn't lose you. It wasn't me.

TUPPER: I'm trying.

FORESKIN: Don't. You're too earnest. That frightens me, I want to run and hide in frivolity. Earnest sincerity constrains this country. Whatever we do, it'll never amount to anything more than a mere hiccough in the belch of progress. Tell me some glorious lies.

TUPPER: You didn't pass. You lost us the fucken game.

FORESKIN: That's not bad for starters.

TUPPER: You dodge through half their team. Only one man to beat, three men in support outside you. Why did you try to beat that man? Why didn't you pass? What the hell were you trying for?

FORESKIN: An abstract concept Tupper. Perfection.

TUPPER: Perfection be damned! We could have won the fucken game!

FORESKIN: There's another one next week. Imagine if it had come off.

TUPPER: Imagination be fucked! You should have passed!

FORESKIN: To pass or not to pass. I pass.

TUPPER: This is important. It's important that we thrash it out. For the sake of the team.

FORESKIN: Everything's important Tupper. And equally futile. Your team, my ingrown toe-nail, grants from government and pillow pennies from the fairies. And why Kenny's in a coma in hospital. Can you follow my lack of reason? That's important. Sincerely, earnestly, if necessary.

TUPPER: It's a man's game.

FORESKIN: Funny, Ken seemed to have most of the physical characteristics. Was there a mystical something that he lacked?

TUPPER: Not a question of that. Good lad, Ken. Certain reservations about his captaincy but . . . you've got to be fit enough to take the knocks.

FORESKIN: What's fitness got to do with saving you from a kick in the head? The only ones who are immune to that are the ones with their brains already scrambled. Like Clean.

TUPPER: Clean did a good job out there today. In fact, to be quite honest, when Kenny went off and Clean took over the captaincy, he lifted our whole game.

FORESKIN: That's not the only thing he lifted out there today Tupper.

TUPPER: Whaddayamean?

FORESKIN: You see a lot from my position Tupper. Pity you didn't let Clean in on your omniscient guarantees of safety to Ken.

TUPPER: Whaddayamean?

FORESKIN: I mean it's funny. Like a criminal dressed as a cop is funny, and brutality legalised by a referee's whistle is absolutely hilarious. That Kenny got kicked in the head twice by the same player, yet we were playing different teams each time — well, that really takes the cake. Do you see how truly funny that is?

TUPPER: I see what you fucken-well mean. That it was Clean kicked his own skipper in the head. Whaddaya suggesting? Who the fuck do you think you are? Whaddarya, eh? What the fuck are ya? What your fucken generation needs is a fucken good war to straighten you out.

FORESKIN: We got Choice instead. That's as much of a trial for most of us. Besides, I would have thought shooting your own superior in the back was frowned upon even in the best of bloody good wars.

FORESKIN *goes to leave.* TUPPER *goes to stop* FORESKIN, *catching him by the arm.*

TUPPER: Hang on, wait, wait . . . How is the lad?
FORESKIN: No change, still in a coma the last time I rang.

Pause

TUPPER: He didn't, did he? It wasn't Clean?

Pause. LARRY *enters, worried.*

LARRY: Seymour. Telephone — someone from the hospital.
FORESKIN: Jesus.

    FORESKIN *exits with* LARRY, *leaving* TUPPER *alone.*

TUPPER: Clean. Clean. Clean! Clean you fucking bastard!

    TUPPER *takes off his sportscoat and throws it on a chair.* CLEAN, *shadowy, comes down from TV light.*

CLEAN: Yeah Tee. What's the guts?
TUPPER: Ken. Ken!

    CLEAN *shrugs.*

CLEAN: Accident.
TUPPER: Twice!
CLEAN: Accidents happen.

    CLEAN'S *brazenness takes* TUPPER *aback. He stares, taking it all in. He nods slowly, then softly to himself.*

TUPPER: Fool. What a fucken fool.

Pause

You. You're the scrapings from someone's grot. You low scum.

Harder

Traitor! You're a fucken traitor!

    TUPPER *swings wildly at* CLEAN, *misses, and stumbles into him.* CLEAN *initially tries simply to restrain* TUPPER *in a boxer's clinch, but* TUPPER *is intent on mayhem and rips* CLEAN *to the belly.* CLEAN *grunts and, now enraged, throws* TUPPER *back against the wall. He follows* TUPPER *to the wall, catches him by the throat as he rebounds from the wall.* CLEAN *straightens* TUPPER *back up against the wall, withdraws his right hand from* TUPPER'S *throat, and draws it back.*

CLEAN: You fucken stupid old fart, you'll get yours!

LARRY *has entered, terribly distressed. He rushes over, tries to break between* TUPPER *and* CLEAN, *coming in from* CLEAN'S *left.*

LARRY: Leave him! Please leave him! No more!

CLEAN *changes slightly the trajectory of his right hand, so that it crosses on to* LARRY'S *jaw.* LARRY *falls backwards and lies still.* TUPPER *has almost broken free, afraid now, trying only to escape.* CLEAN *turns his attention back to* TUPPER, *catches him, pins him back against the wall, draws his right fist back again.* FORESKIN *rushes in, carrying an empty bottle. He begins screaming as he raises the bottle, aiming it at* CLEAN *and* TUPPER. *At the last moment, he turns and dashes the bottle full force into the television tube, shattering both. Silence.*

FORESKIN *initially addresses* CLEAN *and* TUPPER *and those who were supposedly watching the television, but as he progresses, he moves downstage so that he is addressing himself to the theatre audience.*

To some extent the final monologue should be a parody of CLEAN'S *opening speech, but the dominant emotions in* FORESKIN *are anger, sorrow, anguish.*

FORESKIN: Gentlemen. Lads. Boys. Unaccustomed as I am to the customs here, unaccustomed as I am to the . . . small ethics of the situation, or to death, dying, obituaries, eulogies, wakes, kicks, comas or . . . dear, dead friends — there, I've said it plain enough. He's dead plain enough, Ken. And that ought to be a finish, an end to it, surely. But I'm unaccustomed to leaving questions unasked — I've never measured my questions by the possibility of answers. So I ask: why? why? Oh, in the asking I realise that I'm putting a dash after his death, making a pathetic demand for continuity in place of the natural void. I'm sorry, almost. I'm so unaccustomed to being . . . unaccustomed.

I suppose we really ought to do this right: sing 'For He's a Jolly Good Fellow' and 'It's the way we do it in the army, the navy and on the football field' — he was a jolly good fellow. Ask the lads, the boys, to form a ruck at the side of his grave, rake earth over him with their sprigs, make a wreath of dirty laces, and ask the ladies to bring a tear — would that I could, but like most of you, us, we were taught not to cry a vale of tears ago. We'll thank the referee, or the god almighty, he might have made a bad fist of it, we can't understand some of his decisions, but, lord, it's a tough game, a game still, for men, for men called boys.

I was born of the same mothers as you — all! I was part of a whole generation that grew up on wintry mornings running from between mum's warm coat ends on to dewy green fields that seemed as vast as the Russian steppes. And we'd swarm, this way and that, the ball a nominal focus, and the rows of earnest parents our sidelines, having no idea of how to score, how to win, or lose, or even which way to run if we got the ball, except away . . . from all that attention. But even then, ambition wasn't far away, we could feel it rising in steam-breath from the screaming side-line mouths — Kill him!

There were times of closeness, father and son, brother and weary brother, waking very early on cold mornings, huddling together under a blanket in front of a wireless waiting for it . . . wait for it, wait for it! — and for a whole generation god was only twice as high as the posts.

We who know our history by itineraries — the cold war of the '50s you say? Oh yes, we remember it well, those front-row problems, Skinner and Bekker. '59? A melange of O'Reilly's creamy thighs, Jackson's jink, DB's size 13s, and a sheep-dog retrieving the ball in a cow-paddock in Morrinsville. Froggies in '61, Poms again in '66 — bloody awful! — those artistes of '68 Villepreux and Jo Maso, a Pinetree bestriding the '60s with a sheep under each arm, the Bokkies in '73 — the ones that didn't come, that never more will come. The old order never would have changèd. We were DBed, JJed, BGed, jardened, cooked, nicholled, elvidged, fred allenned, otagoed in '49, bayed through the '60s, and through all of it, hot and cold wars, '51 strikes, recessions, depressions and the booms that gave them depth, hippies, yippies, and all the determined dog-paddling through our little backwater, there was one thing we knew with certainty: come winter, we'd be there, on the terrace, answering the only call that mattered — c'mon black!

Then, later, a lot older, slower, more in need, standing on bare boards in cigarette smoke, a cold sausage roll in one hand and a warm jug of beer in the other, listening once again to one for the ref and one for the ladies' plates. And an arthritic future to look forward to in the myths of old, criticisms of new; while the nectar flowed till you could almost see the reflection of your youth in its dregs . . . passing . . . passing.

I know the lore. I know the catechism. It's funny. I look at you all. I was born of the same mothers as you. And now . . . I'm wondering what happened after that. Why am I now so . . . unaccustomed?

Oh, I escaped from all that — I think that's probably where I left you. I went from here and wandered . . . I seem to have wandered drunken through that life, sometimes vital and frothy as a jug, sometimes slack-jawed and despondent, sometimes almost . . . original! Tortilla-flatted in the university ghetto; winoed the night under cherry trees too cold to blossom, butch cassidy bi-cycled buxom blonde bergen birds, arse on handlebars . . . and, intellectually . . . awakened —
bellowed at, barthed, pynched on, coovered into submission
my words
my life
parenthesised.
Calvined at conception
a press-ganged preterite
what could I possibly say that was original
write that was not already Khayamed
pray that was not already pregato